THE LAURENTIANS

Painters in a Landscape

Organized and circulated
by the Art Gallery of Ontario
Extension Services 1977-1978

Mela Constantinidi
Exhibition Producer
Art Gallery of Ontario

Helen Duffy
Consultant

Distributed in Canada by
Gage Publishing Limited
and Les Editions Internationales
Alain Stanké

Contents

cover:

55. Goodridge Roberts
Landscape, Morin Heights, 1953
oil on masonite
32 x 45 in. 81.28 x 114.3 cm.

Foreword

The Extension Services Branch of the Art Gallery of Ontario is justifiably proud of this exhibition which has been almost two years in planning. From the very beginning, the response to this show was unusually enthusiastic. The exhibition coincides with the revival in popularity of some of the Montreal painters associated with the Laurentians, such as Edwin Holgate, Goodridge Roberts and Marc-Aurèle Fortin. We were supported and helped by the living artists, the artists' families, many institutions, commercial galleries and private lenders. Their personal involvement contributed greatly to the project.

I would like to take this opportunity to thank all those whose interest and co-operation made the project possible. First and foremost we must thank the National Museums Corporation for their financial assistance in both the organizational phase and the costs of moving the show from centre to centre. After its tour in Canada the exhibition will have its final showing at the Canadian Cultural Centre in Paris, France. The catalogue is printed in both English and French editions.

Special thanks are due to Helen Duffy who has acted as the special consultant to the show and whose long-standing association with the Quebec art movement and familiarity with the Laurentians prompted her to approach us with this idea. Also to be thanked is Robert Ayre, well-known writer and art critic, who agreed to write our introduction with a very personal approach.

We must especially thank Mela Constantinidi, Exhibition Producer, whose dedicated efforts brought this show together.

Finally, of course, we extend our special thanks to the lenders for without their generosity the show would not have been possible.

William J. Withrow
Director

Preface and Acknowledgements

Over the past years, the Laurentian area north of Montreal has attracted many artists interested in interpreting a landscape which has its own unique character. Our exhibition theme covers the past fifty years although painters, photographers and others explored the area well before the 1920s. It includes paintings, drawings, sketches and prints by artists who have lived and worked there, and who experienced a special affinity towards the region. The exhibition shows how they viewed this landscape and demonstrates the diversity of their personal interpretations.

During the preparation of the exhibition, we have been helped and encouraged by many people, and we would especially like to thank Mr. and Mrs. Jean Allaire, Madeleine Arbour S.D.E., Mr. and Mrs. Robert Ayre, Harold Beament R.C.A., Paul Beaulieu, Françoise Côté, Mr. and Mrs. Timothy Creery, John Fox, Robert Hall, Allan Harrison, Mr. and Mrs. John Langdon, Mr. and Mrs. Jean Paul Lemieux, T.R. MacDonald, R.C.A., Linda McKnight, Eric McLean, Bernard Morisset S.D.E., Guy Robert, Françoise Sullivan, Philip Surrey, Gabor Szilasi, Mrs. William R. Watson, Claire Watson, Herbert Whittaker, and Basil Zarov, who, in their own individual ways, have all contributed towards the realization of the exhibition.

We would like to express our appreciation for the personal cooperation of Frances K. Smith, Agnes Etherington Art Centre, Queen's University, Kingston, Ontario; Michel Champagne and Yvon Milliard, Musée du Québec; Charles C. Hill, The National Gallery of Canada, Ottawa; Simon Dresdnere, Toronto; and in Montreal, Leah Sherman, Concordia University, Conrad E.W. Graham and Stanley G. Triggs, McCord Museum; Germain Lefèbvre and Micheline Moisan, The Montreal Museum of Fine Arts; Gilles Corbeil, Claude Gadoury, Paul Kastel, Eric Klinkhoff, and Dr. Max Stern.

We extend our thanks to the many members of the Art Gallery of Ontario staff who have helped in the smooth running of the exhibition's organization and its accompanying catalogue, especially Diane Vetere, Assistant to the Exhibition Producer.

But the exhibition has only been made possible through the magnanimity of the lenders which we gratefully acknowledge, and the active participation and assistance of the artists themselves and their families. We sincerely thank Mr. and Mrs. André Biéler, Mrs. Judith Borenstein and Joyce Borenstein, Mrs. Mieze Brandtner, Mrs. Brooke Claxton, Mr. and Mrs. John B. Claxton, Mr. and Mrs. Edwin Holgate, Patrick Landsley, Mrs. T.W.L. MacDermot, Mr. and Mrs. Robert McDougall, Louis Muhlstock, Roland and Suzanne Pichet, Jean-Paul Riopelle, Mrs. Joan Roberts, and Jacques de Tonnancour.

M.C. and H.D.

1 Bird's-eye view
  Ste Agathe des Monts (Lac des Sables)

Introduction

————

The rugged, lake-sprinkled Laurentian mountains and hills northwest of Montreal reach up to the border of the Canadian Shield, also known as the Grenville Province, which runs north-eastward from Lake Huron for 2000 km. to the coast of Labrador, covering an area of 4,000,000 square km. Geological surveys tell us that the formation of the rocky landscape had been fully developed between 1750 and 1900 million years ago.

Our exhibition theme is concerned only with one small area which through its proximity to Montreal has attracted artists over the past five decades. *Laurentian* paintings have been widely exhibited in group or one-man exhibitions, in private galleries and museum collections. Usually no particular distinction is made between the various areas linked to the Laurentian mountain range. And yet, the Laurentians north of Montreal differ greatly from the Laurentians stretching down past Quebec towards the Gaspé where the sky dominates the land and the St. Lawrence river bed widens on its way to the sea until one can only see the other shore on very clear days.

In the words of André Biéler, who lived and painted in both areas:

The great order of the St. Lawrence landscape below Quebec is evident. The river flows between two sets of hills, the greater ones to the north, and as the hills modulate and flow, parallel to the river, the whole landscape and the civilization that was built on those shores are conditioned by this parallelism. Roads are always either parallel, or at right angles – the right angled roads are the montées, *and these are the roads that seem to climb and disappear, and appear again in the distance, the road well drawn by the rail fences on both sides. The hills are a series of parallel ridges. But just as soon as you go on the other road, the* rangs, *then the landscape changes; you are running parallel to the mountains and undulate in another way.*

But when you change from this natural geographic fact, which is dominant there, to the mountainous border of the Canadian shield north of Montreal, then you come upon another type of landscape altogether. A much more chaotic, a much more haphazard flowing of hills together. They do, of course, border la Rivière du Nord, which flows down from the hills, but not in that very definite fashion of the lower St. Lawrence. And there you come upon a very different kind of landscape, a landscape of hills that give the artist almost more of a chance to arrange them in an interesting way on the canvas, but to finish with not so forcible a design as found in the lower St. Lawrence region. That is why there is more variety in the landscapes of the Laurentian painters in the lower St. Lawrence.[1]

In restricting this exhibition to one region only, to what may look, on the map, not unlike an artificially enclosed garden, we attempt to show how different artists at different times over the past fifty years viewed the same landscape and the various ways they interpreted it.

For every one of the painters represented, the Laurentians north of Montreal were or are a chosen environment. Within this environment they expressed, in a variety of media, the essence of their individual discoveries.

The painter in the landscape is at all times surrounded by his subject. It is inescapably there, a studio without walls. The changeable conditions of open air, the awareness of atmospheric changes as the sun, the clouds moving across the sky subordinate or emphasize forms, shapes, masses, tonalities and distances, require an artist to work spontaneously and with flexibility. According to his temperament and his sensitivity he identifies with what he sees before and around him. At the same time the memory of moments of seeing in the past, experiences of touching, discovering, understanding, and the powerful and ever present world of the inner landscape become part of his concentration.

At this moment he also is contemporary, expresses imperceptibly a contemporary concept of his own time sense. This awareness stretches well beyond the prevalent tastes of his own society, the acceptance or rejection of present and past art forms.

Maurice Cullen, on his first visit to Mont Tremblant in 1912, discovered the region which was to become the passionate love of his life later on. Jean-Paul Riopelle explored it in his early youth. Both were to return, after years of travel and living abroad, to establish studios. Their chosen environment led to quite different interpre-

[1]Interview with Frances K. Smith, Kingston, September 26, 1976

tations: for Cullen, the relentless obsession with the landscape of fact unfolding again and again the harmonious curve of the Caché River; for Riopelle, the prismatic approach fusing a myriad of visual impressions.

Some of the works in this exhibition were not unanimously accepted by the public or the critics. In some cases they were indeed roundly rejected and the artist's sincerity not only put in doubt but ridiculed.

As it happens anywhere in the world, where artists discover the visual properties of secluded or unknown regions and open the eyes of a public, even in the face of opposition – the artist will be followed by the seeker of the "unspoilt and beautiful." The development of recreation and tourist centres, encouraged by the residents for economic reasons, brings also the invasion of the "fashion painters" who with much temperament and sentimentality depict the objective facts of nature.

"Laurentianizing" became the rage in the thirties and forties, reflecting beliefs and modes of expression aimed at evoking feelings of nostalgia by seductive banality. The studio-created winterscenes with imaginary mountain peaks could, in the absence of a typical French Canadian homestead, just as well represent Norway or Switzerland. They are still a standard feature decoration in rural inns, motels and private homes, accepted and ignored. Their popularity, however, together with the popularity of the landscape itself with its expanding urbanization, accounts for a conscious rejection of the area by a number of landscape painters in Quebec who turned to the more gentle rural areas of the Eastern Townships south-east of Montreal.

The fifteen painters represented in this exhibition had and have an intimate and affectionate relationship with the Laurentian region in the north. We have tried in the biographies, and other material used in text and illustrations of this catalogue, to underline the individuality of each artist in order to emphasize the fact that, though close friendships existed between many of them, the choice of place, time, subject and media was always a matter of personal preference.

Mela Constantinidi and Helen Duffy

5. André Biéler
Horses and Sleigh, c. 1931
conté on paper
5¼ x 7 in.   13.4 x 17.8 cm.

12. *Voting at Ste Adèle*, 1937
ink and watercolour on card
5½ x 6¼ in.   13.8 x 15.8 cm.

4. *St Sauveur*, c. 1931
conté on paper
5¼ x 7 in.   13.4 x 17.7 cm.

10. *St Sauveur*, 1932
coloured crayon on paper
7 x 10½ in.   17.8 x 26.5 cm.

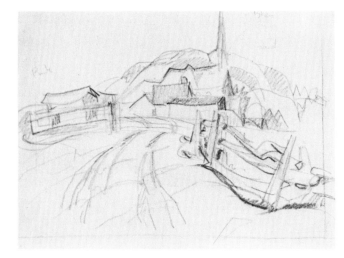

We discovered the Laurentians soon after we moved to Montreal from Winnipeg nearly fifty years ago. As it happened, we never went back to the hotel at Weir where we enjoyed the weekend – not because we weren't satisfied with our first choice, but because there was no need for hotels as we came to know the mountains and the lakes intimately over the years. We stayed with friends, or in cottages they lent us, or at *pensions* or boarding houses – like Royanna, on its own miniature lake at St Calixte de Kilkenny, near Lac Achigan, Otter Lake House, at the end of the railway line, and Watchorn's farm at Morin Heights.

In the days before we had a car, we travelled by railway. We were no skiers, so we never went north on the ski trains that were once so popular with singing young people, before the railway disappeared from the mountains. The other seasons we knew well, however, from blackfly time through the summer to the pageantry of fall, and we became familiar with the landmarks along the CNR line between St Jérome and Huberdeau.

We rented cottages by the season in the forties and fifties. The first, at Patry's Bay on far-spreading Bark Lake, a long taxi ride from the station at Arundel, demanded the pioneering spirit because up there in those days we depended on oil lamps and my wife Thelma pasteurized the milk on the wood stove. On the first night, we wrapped ourselves in the curtains and in the blankets lent us by a neighbour because the truck failed to arrive with our baggage and bedding. We had the lake and the boat, the pitcher plants in the swamp – remembered as we remember the giant mulleins at Royanna – the fragrant wild roses, the raspberries, the blueberries – fruit and foliage – the goldenrod and asters in their time, the crickets on the sun-stunned meadow, and the whip-poor-wills at dusk, calling the moon to come up over the rock, and the stars, never more brilliant than at chilly five a.m., when I had to be up to get the train back to town.

The Igloo was closer to civilization, a log cabin in the woods on one of the Echo lakes, a short walk to Morin Heights. We had a fireplace, electricity, and ice in a refrigerator instead of under the verandah floor.

1951 there was the summer of the mushroom, because I had been sent Dr. René Pomerleau's book for review, for the sake of the superb drawings by A.Y. Jackson's brother Harry. (His portrait *The Naturalist*, painted by Edwin Holgate in 1941, is in the Musée du Québec.) Our life was enlarged by the search for chanterelles, agarics, the boletus, the russula and other fungi, both edible and deadly. We even found the Destroying Angel. A reader sent me a stinkhorn, which is one way of showing a critic what you think of him.

One of our most memorable experiences of the Laurentians was in winter, when we were guests at a New Year's Eve party in St Sauveur. The centre was André Biéler's cottage on the main street – *en face de Mme David* – with André's 1931 fresco of St Christopher spread across the front – a wayside shrine for skiers: "Whoever seeth this image shall not faint or fall today. *Regardes à St Christophe et t'en va rassuré.*"

We ate at Mme David's – I remember the rich home-made *pâté* – and had the run of the house to play Murder, the popular game of the time. Most of the party slept there, but I was one of those who spent the night in the cottage. I don't say I slept because André managed to get the ancient clock started to bring in the New Year. It struck 12 all right but, as if it enjoyed its voice after so long a silence, it went on striking. When, after I don't know how many bongs, it finally subsided, the wooden works kept up their loud wooden click-clack all night.

The next day, while the others skied, we walked to Morin Heights – the road was clear. We were always hikers.

We stayed with John and Corinne Lyman at St Jovite. Even before he organized the Eastern Group, as a rival to the Group of Seven, and the Contemporary Arts Society, to spread the gospel of "true painting" – *belle peinture* – to the wider lay public, Lyman was the elder statesman, who had his salon and who liked to meet and encourage young people, though he afterwards came to believe that some of them let him down and he grew vindictive with a bitterness and violence that shocked some of us who thought we knew him.

One of the young painters was Goodridge Roberts and it was when Lyman lent him the cottage that he

iii St Jovite, 1939
L to R: John Lyman,
Goodridge Roberts,
Fritz Brandtner

came to know the Laurentians and began painting what he considered his first good landscapes in oils. And Roberts went on to influence the landscape painting of Jacques de Tonnancour and Jean Paul Lemieux, though of course they went on to develop their own individual vision.

Lyman was a Canadian, born in New England, but he became a European and even said, "Every real painter is a Latin insofar as he is a painter." Back in Montreal, the Lymans were so homesick for Europe that I remember Corinne saying, in hushed reverence, when there was a lot of flu around Montreal, "They have it over there too."

They were exiles from Europe, but though Corinne was a French-Canadian, John couldn't make himself a Latin and sometimes he had doubts about himself as a painter.

He learned something from Matisse, though it was never clear to me how close his association with him was. As a painter – certainly in the Laurentian landscape – he had his Anglo-Saxon reserves and inhibitions – even though he was trounced by the critics when he first exhibited at home in Canada. The terrible S. Morgan-Powell blamed Matisse for his bad influence: "If Montreal joins London and laughs," he wrote, "the craze will soon pass."

Lyman's Laurentian landscapes are stilted, self-consciously *composed,* as compared with those of painters like Fritz Brandtner and Sam Borenstein, who let themselves go. Brandtner would transmute the landscape according to his own driving and inventive energy. Yet he was a disciplined designer. Borenstein was a natural force, who threw himself almost furiously into the landscape, so impetuously that organization might be a matter of chance.

A robust and dynamic painter, Anne Savage's wielding of big masses and powerful rhythms revealed the undomesticated Laurentians that belonged to the greater Canada. She was closer to the Group of Seven than the eighth member, Edwin Holgate, who was, with all his strong feeling for the landscape, more the figure painter. His neighbour in Morin Heights, Peter Whalley, in his takeoff of the Group and the Pine Tree, recognizes his theme of the nude in the landscape: Holgate "introduces group therapy."

Lyman didn't get excited over the landscape and he suspected those who did. Of course he scorned the Group for its brashness. So did many other Canadians, conservatives who were offended by these upstarts having the effrontery to "shoot holes in the Dutch," as Alec Jackson said they were doing, and loyal citizens like the Prime Minister, Mackenzie King, who feared they would be bad for immigration.

But the insurrectionists shared a spirit of adventure, excitement in the discovery of a Canada unexploited by the painters, and they had an urge to celebrate. People began to respond, recognizing the excitement as reflecting the excitement they felt themselves, when it was pointed out to them. The "hot mush"[1] gibe didn't bother them.

Montreal's playground in the mountains north of the city is more domestic than the country discovered by the Group. The invasion of a marginal farming country by the city folk looking for a playground, setting up children's camps, and "fresh air" resorts for the underprivileged, building hotels, summer cottages and ski chalets, and some more pretentious establishments, goes back a long way in the history of Quebec. Trails were developed for cross-country skiers, ski-tows were erected – sometimes artificial snow was provided. Men came to fish and hunt,

[1]H.F. Gadsby, "The Hot Mush School – or – Peter and I," *The Toronto Daily Star,* December 12, 1913.

boys living in camps like the YMCA's Kanawana slept in tents and ventured on over-night canoe trips.

The painters of the Laurentians didn't have to be explorers and woodsmen to discover the country. And there was no group making common cause, nothing that could be taken as nationalism, no celebration that could make news and become a cult.

Families settled in for the summer, going north as early as the blackflies let them – or risking them – and staying until school opened or winter insisted it was time to shut off the water and close up. People began living in the Laurentians the year round, some of them daily commuters to the city.

Fritz Brandtner did much of his Laurentian painting when he was teaching at the social service settlement camp for slum children at Sixteen Island Lake. Louis Muhlstock has been going up to the family farm Isola at Val David for many seasons, painting the hills in all weathers and looking closely and lovingly at the wildflowers and grasses, the birds and animals, domestic and wild, alive and dead.

Anne Savage lived in her own cottage at Lake Wonish above Sixteen Island Lake and used it as her head-quarters for sorties farther afield.

Permanent residents we know included the ceramist Claude Vermette and his wife the tapestry weaver Mariette Rousseau, at Ste Adèle, the sculptor Gord Smith, at Lake Macdonald, and H.W. Jones at St Sauveur. With the sculptors must be mentioned Peter Whalley, the satirist in cartoons whose irreverent history of Canadian painting *Northern Blights* was published by his Upbank Press at Morin Heights in 1972. He brings the same mischie-vous genius to the figures he is making out of old can openers and other found objects.

The longest established painter in the Laurentians was of course Edwin Holgate. He had painted there as early as 1923, when he built a shack at Lac Tremblant, and in 1945 he and his wife Frances settled in the house he had built near Morin Heights.

One of his best stories is about how he sold his Montreal house on Lorne Avenue. He asked for cash and the purchaser took him literally and arrived with bundles of bills, hoarded so long that some of them smelled musty. Holgate was aghast and he dug up his gun and kept vigil all night. The next day he made it to the bank, without being followed, the money distributed in his clothing, and unburdened himself in the safety of the manager's office.

Edwin and Frances stayed at Morin Heights for twenty-nine years, until in 1974, on the doctor's advice, they took an apartment in the city.

Dennis Reid, in his biography in the Canadian Artists series, speaks of the "isolated life," but though his visits to Montreal and his exhibitions became more and more infrequent, Holgate took his part in the community life of Morin Heights and the activities of the Canadian Legion, and he went on painting – portraits like that of "Uncle George" Watchorn and many small landscapes in which he revealed the more intimate aspects of the mountains with affectionate lyricism.

The most recent arrival I know of in the Laurentians is Jean-Paul Riopelle. We remember our delight in recognizing the Canadian landscape in his great abstractions at the Venice Biennale in 1962, but we have not seen the painting and drawing he has been doing since he converted the big barn at Lac Masson into a studio in 1974. He comes since our time in the Laurentians. Whether he will stay is a question. When Laurent Lamy asked him if he intended to root himself anew in Quebec, he said he did not believe in taking root anywhere.

Robert Ayre was joint editor for *Canadian Art* magazine, 1944-1959, and art critic for the *Montreal Star*, 1950-1970. He has written numerous articles, essays and short stories.

43 . a Roland Pichet

Suite Québecoise: blues pour un piquet de clôture, 1975
serigraph
13 x 20 in. 33.02 x 50.8 cm.

14. **André Biéler**
Election Day, Ste Adèle, 1938
watercolour on paper
19³/₈ x 24¹/₈ in.   49.21 x 61.28 cm.

20. Fritz Brandtner
Fall, n.d.
watercolour on paper
$19^{1}/_{2}$ x $24^{1}/_{8}$ in.   49.5 x 61.3 cm.

24. **Marc-Aurèle Fortin**
Pastorale, 1928
watercolour
23 x 27⁶/₁₀ in.   58 x 70 cm.

25. Marc-Aurèle Fortin
Vue de Lesage, Laurentides, c. 1938
oil on canvas
51¹⁄₈ x 67 in. 130 x 170 cm.

55. Goodridge Roberts
Landscape, Morin Heights, 1953
oil on masonite
32 x 45 in.   81.28 x 114.3 cm.

58. **Anne Savage**
July, Wonish, 1960
oil on masonite
33 x 48 in.   83.82 x 121.92 cm.

27. **Edwin Holgate**
Morin Heights, 1927
oil on board
11 x 16 in. 27.94 x 40.64 cm.

39. **Louis Muhlstock**
Laurentian Interior, Val Morin, 1938
oil on canvas
26 x 30 in. 66.04 x 76.2 cm.

59. **Jacques de Tonnancour**
Paysage de juin, 1957
oil on panel
31¼ x 43¾ in.   79.4 x 111.1 cm.

47. Jean-Paul Riopelle
Untitled, 1974
oil on canvas
57½ x 38¼ in. 146.05 x 97.16 cm.

34. Patrick Landsley
   Winter Light, 1973
   oil and acrylic on canvas
   69 x 54 in. 175.26 x 137.16 cm.

photo: Frances K. Smith, December 1971

André Biéler   1896 –

André Biéler was born October 8, 1896, in Lausanne, the third of five sons of Rev. Charles Biéler. Soon afterwards the family moved to Paris. He comes from a Swiss family distinguished in the liberal arts and theology. His father was a Protestant theologian, his grandfather a noted historian of the Reformation. His uncle was the well-known Swiss painter Ernest Biéler.

The formative influence of a family environment strong in traditional, intellectual and artistic values was further enriched by his childhood education at the Lycée Carnot where art instruction was an important subject.

When André's father was appointed Professor of Theology and Registrar of the Presbyterian College in Montreal in 1908, the family moved to Canada.

The total disregard of art as a subject in the Quebec school system at that time was a frustrating personal experience for the twelve-year-old Biéler. It led him towards pioneer projects in art education later in his life.

In 1913 he entered a preparatory course in architecture at McGill University. He broke off his academic career two years later to enlist with the First University Company Princess Patricia's Canadian Light Infantry.

In World War I he was wounded at Sanctuary Wood in 1916. In 1917 he left the regiment, being badly gassed at the battle of Passchendaele.

His transfer to the Canadian Army headquarters, Topographical Section, as a map draughtsman with the rank of sergeant, brought him in close contact with art-oriented staff members and with visiting Canadian war artists.

Though his health was deteriorating, he became head of the section. At the end of the war, Biéler was physically exhausted. His convalescence made extended stays in southern climates necessary. He studied for a few months at the Fine Arts Department of Stetson University, Florida, and then in 1920 with the Art Students' League at Woodstock, N.Y. Back in Montreal he could not settle down.

In October 1921 he returned to Europe to study at the Ecole du Louvre and the Atelier Ranson, with Maurice Denis and Paul Serusier, in Paris. He travelled extensively. From his uncle, Ernest Biéler, known for his understanding and love for mountain people and their lives, he learned every aspect of technique in the domain of true fresco while working on murals for the Town Hall of LeLocle in the Swiss Jura Mountains.

His own paintings of this period were shown in one-man exhibitions, *Scènes et Paysages Suisses,* at the

Art Association of Montreal in 1924 and in Geneva, Switzerland, two years later.

André Biéler came back to Canada in 1926 and lived on the Isle of Orleans near Quebec City to record in both drawing and painting the life of the farm people around him. "For a time I was satisfied with the mirroring of a certain civilization which was fast disappearing," Andre reflects, "I realized it was disappearing, this provincial thing in Quebec, and I was keen to bring it forth."[1]

When, at 34, he felt ready for a more diverse way of life he returned to Montreal. First at a studio on Ste Famille Street in the house of the sculptor Laliberté, then at Beaver Hall Hill, he quickly made contact with city realities in times of economic depression.

In partnership with John Lyman and other artists he taught at the "Atelier." With interior decorator and designer Jeannette Meunier, whom he married in 1931, he extended his activities into the field of theatre and costume design, furniture and interiors, fabric and posters and, in collaboration with spinners and weavers in the lower St. Lawrence region, promoted the use of homespun textiles in interior decoration.

In St Sauveur the Biélers had found a tiny pioneer house on the main street which became more and more their refuge from hectic city activities. Here André would take part, sketchbook in hand, in the local festivities: "They were not sketches of the subject painter, hurrying to a picturesque spot, making a quick sketch and going home. It is only after walking through the hills, meeting people, getting acquainted with the village life, that the essence of such an environment could be grasped."[2]

By 1935 the Biélers were ready to move permanently to the Laurentians. The commercial work in Montreal, no matter how financially rewarding, had become too demanding. Again, in André Biéler's words: "We chose St Adèle because of its location, a lovely unspoilt village. We had a house, and living in the village was very reasonable, and it was just an ideal situation. We got there in the spring and I can remember immediately going out sketching, enjoying the new-found freedom, and feeling that this was going to be my destination."[3]

But two months later word from Queen's University challenged these dreams with an offer for Biéler to create an art department, to teach art within the University curriculum and some studio courses for the community in Kingston. Though the Biélers returned often to the Laurentians and the close link with the area remained, Kingston was to be their permanent home from September 1936 onward.

In 1940 on a teaching assignment on the west coast, he conceived the idea for a get-together of artists, and in June, the following year, 150 delegates assembled from all parts of Canada for the first Conference of Canadian Artists. The Federation of Canadian Artists was formed with André Biéler as its first president.

He developed the Summer School of Painting at Queen's and became a lecturer much in demand in other parts of Canada.

His fundamental love for people, his basic awareness of community needs and the integration of art in contemporary society are reflected in other work as well as in his paintings and prints. His large murals for the Aluminum Company at Shipshaw 1945; Veteran's Building, Ottawa, 1955; Chalmers United Church Kingston, 1958, among others, still set standards of quality and taste and show at the same time the artist's wide range of technical skill. He expresses himself in a variety of media: casein, oil, acrylic, tempera, watercolour; woodcut, *pochoir*, intaglio and sculpture, stimulated by the work of his son, Ted Bieler. He designed and built The Twelve Pines Press on pneumatic principles in 1968.

Since 1936 André Biéler has had one-man exhibitions in Kingston, Montreal, Toronto, Winnipeg and San Miguel de Allende, Mexico, and his work has been included in important national and international exhibitions in Paris, London, Chicago, Boston and Rio de Janeiro. His paintings can be found in many important private and public collections. The 1970 retrospective exhibition spanning fifty years of the artist's work was organized and circulated by the Agnes Etherington Art Centre, Queen's University, Kingston.

An Associate of the Royal Academy since 1942, he was elected a full member in 1955. He also belongs to the Ontario Society of Artists, the Canadian Society of Painters in Water Colour and the Canadian Society of Graphic Art. In 1967 he was awarded the Centennial Medal for Service to Canada, and two years later an honorary Doctorate of Laws degree from Queen's University.

[1] from tape recording with Peter Harcourt for the film *Biéler*, 1972/73

[2] from a tape recording with Frances K. Smith, Kingston, September 29, 1976

[3] from a tape recording with Frances K. Smith, Kingston, February 11, 1972

1. André Biéler
Early Spring in the Laurentians, 1929
oil on canvas
20 x 26¼ in. 50.8 x 66.7 cm.

Sam Borenstein   1908 - 1969

Sam Borenstein was born in Suwalki, Poland on January 15, 1908. When he was thirteen the family came to Canada and settled in Montreal. As a young man, he worked at various jobs, mainly in the fur and garment industries, and became a garment cutter by trade. He was virtually a self-taught artist, although he studied over a period of three years at the Monument National with Elzear Soucy, a professor of sculpture and wood carving.

Borenstein began painting in his spare time until he became so absorbed by it that he gave up his job to concentrate entirely on art. He travelled to Paris in 1939, and spent almost a year studying and painting there and in Brittany.

His works were exhibited frequently during the late thirties: at the Art Association of Montreal's Annual Spring Exhibition, March 1937; at the New York World's Fair in 1939. That same year he had a one-man exhibition at the Fine Art Galleries of the T. Eaton Company, Toronto, where he was to exhibit several times. His most common subjects then were bouquets or vases of flowers and scenes of Montreal, in bright, vivid, sometimes startling colour. At a later exhibition at the same galleries in September 1943, Borenstein included portraits and landscape paintings, and although he was still painting with great vigour, his colours were less violent than before.

About this time Borenstein began spending every summer in the Laurentians and he continued to do so until he died in 1969. During the forties, he stayed at St Donat, then later at Val David; from 1948 to 1955 he was in Shawbridge and Lac Marois and from 1956 to 1969 he spent much of his time at his 'old school house' at Lac Brulé. Apart from these localities which were the origin of many of his paintings, he explored the immediate vicinity, working frequently in and around Ste Lucie, Ste Adèle, Ivry, Piedmont and Mont Rolland. Fellow artists and friends who often accompanied Borenstein included A.Y. Jackson, Ralph Burton, Ernest Newman, and Goodridge Roberts who had known him as a young student.

Borenstein continued to exhibit, mainly in Montreal. On seven occasions he had one-man exhibitions at the Montreal Museum of Fine Arts, Gallery XII – gallery space devoted to the work of local artists; and at the Y.M./Y.W.H.A. Snowdon Building, Montreal, December 1954; the Penthouse Gallery, Montreal, October 1963, and the Walter Klinkhoff Gallery, Montreal, in 1961 and again in 1971.

An exhibition of some 45 works dating from the early thirties to the mid-sixties was shown at the Sir George Williams University Department of Fine Arts, Montreal, in November 1966, and a second important retrospective was held at the Art Gallery of Hamilton, Ontario, in September 1974.

Like many other artists, Sam Borenstein was unable to make a living from his art. In order to supplement his income, he drove a taxicab and traded in antiques. His friends and supporters included Louis Melzack, owner of the Classic Book Shop in Montreal where his works were exhibited regularly, and Joseph Hirshhorn, founder of the Hirshhorn Museum and Sculpture Garden, Smithsonian Institution, Washington, D.C. which now has ten of his paintings in its collection.

In his painting he used various media: oil, gouache, tempera and watercolour, but he preferred oil paint: "It is the hardest medium but it brings good results."[1] He worked with a palette knife as well as brush.

Sam Borenstein has been called an 'expressionist'. His painting has always brought a definite reaction, whether favourable or not, because of his extraordinarily vivid colours, the distortion employed and, perhaps more than anything, because of the emotion which inspired it. He himself thought of his style as "personal realism"[2] and strongly believed that in his landscape painting it was necessary to paint from nature in order to capture its essence.

[1] Sam Borenstein quoted in article by Sheldon Kirshner, *The Westward News*, September 3, 1964
[2] *Ibidem*

Sam Borenstein

...In painting a scene I give it all the energy I have and if
I am not successful at least I tried my best, and will
continue trying. Then, some day you may find secrets are
becoming clear to you, and you realize they are not secrets
but simply things in nature, that are there for you to see.
As you paint and see more, your work becomes fuller.
You combine many years of painting and always add on
to your painting first, enthusiasm, then mood, then
composition, then drawing and form.... Do not try to find
a short cut by imitating other artists' work. Work from
Nature and stick to it. Do not let any one persuade you
that Nature is misleading. All great artists took their
inspiration and their painting from Nature and let that
be a guide. At all times be an artist first, then a technician.

World Affairs, Toronto, December, 1941

16. Sam Borenstein
Village Québecois, 1966
tempera on paper
30 x 40 in.   76.2 x 101.6 cm.

15. Sam Borenstein
Ste Marguerite Station, P.Q., 1943
oil on canvas
28 x 46 in. 71.12 x 116.84 cm.

Fritz Brandtner   1896-1969

Fritz Brandtner spent his early youth in Danzig, a German city–now part of Poland on the Baltic Sea. He was born there in 1896, though the family came originally from Salzburg, Austria.

Danzig was a beautiful city of light and colour, with a fine civic art gallery, where the young Brandtner was able to study the work of the old masters, as well as paintings by such modernists as Hofer, Beckman, Picasso, Modigliani, Grosz and Feininger.

At the outbreak of World War I, Brandtner had to leave school to join the army. He served first on the Russian Front with a cavalry regiment, then in 1916 was transferred to the Western Front where he was taken prisoner by a French patrol. While in prison camp he did many sketches and drawings which he gave to a companion before making an escape attempt, but he never recovered any of them. After serving as a prisoner at forced labour in France following the Armistice, he returned to Danzig in 1920.

The city was economically ruined, but Brandtner found work as a commercial designer. He spent much of his time in the studio of Fritz August Pfuhle, a portrait painter, stained glass worker and Professor at the University of Danzig. Apart from his contact and association with Pfuhle, Brandtner was virtually a self-taught artist. He himself instructed life classes in the Architectural Department of the University from 1924 to 1926.

Post-war Danzig held little future for a young man ambitious to become a creative artist and in 1928 Brandtner emigrated to Canada. He started working in Winnipeg as a housepainter and was then employed by the T. Eaton Company. He was soon joined by his fiancée, Mieze Preuss, and they were married.

It is hardly surprising that Brandtner's painting was received far from enthusiastically in Winnipeg, for his art must have seemed strange indeed to people unfamiliar with new European trends. At his first Canadian exhibition of painting held at the Winnipeg School of Art, in December 1928, his work was roundly condemned by the local art critic. A second one-man show in 1934 was certainly not successful from a sales point of view but the criticism was a little less severe.

One special friend he made during his years in Winnipeg was the painter Lionel Lemoine FitzGerald. The two went on sketching trips together and were known to have exchanged sketches. Encouraged by FitzGerald, the Brandtners moved to Montreal in 1934, where he believed that experimental art would be received more readily than elsewhere in Canada. In Montreal, the Brandtners made their home in a third floor apartment at 1154 Beaver Hall Square where Brandtner lived and painted for the next sixteen years. He worked for some time in the display department of the T. Eaton Company of Montreal, and subsequently as a free-lance designer with the Canadian National Railways and other companies, and undertook several mural commissions.

In February 1936, Dr. Norman Bethune, whom Brandtner had met when Bethune bought one of his paintings, helped organize a one-man exhibition of his works at the Henry Morgan Department Store, sponsored by the Canadian League Against War and Fascism. Brandtner then helped Dr. Bethune set up a Children's Art Centre project in Montreal. Soon after, the doctor left for Spain, but Brandtner continued to support the centre financially and, with Marian Scott, to hold classes for children from poor areas of the city.

Brandtner believed that art should be a vital part of community life, and his classes for children were an outstanding success. He said of his children's art classes: "I am not trying to turn out experts, but to make these children enthusiasts in living…. By expressing themselves in some creative way, they gain a knowledge of higher values which will make life more pleasant and more successful for them."[1] Even so, like so many other painters, he had mixed feelings about the dual role of teacher and artist: "Being an artist and being a teacher are two conflicting things. When I paint my work manifests the

[1]Paul Duval, *Saturday Night*, December 1, 1948

unexpected.... In teaching it is just the opposite. I must account for every line, shape and colour and I am forced to give an explanation of the inexplicable and account for the variety of styles the students present."[2]

From 1949 to 1952, Brandtner spent the summer months as Director of the Observatory Art Centre, University of New Brunswick, Fredericton, where he influenced many by his inspirational teaching.

Brandtner's association with the Laurentians was long-standing. He was attracted by the rough rock formations and the sometimes dramatic quality of the landscape. Many summers he sketched and painted at Sixteen Island Lake and the surrounding areas. Petrified wood shapes, large stones and boulders, trees and leaves often suggested highly abstract forms. In his notebook he said: "I take from Nature what best expresses me. My problem is always to find in Nature communicable formulas, adequate to the expression of my innermost concept."[3] He combined this tendency toward more abstract interpretation of the landscape with his love of bright and vivid colouring. He also taught at a social service settlement camp for underprivileged children located near Sixteen Island Lake, for being in the countryside surrounded by children meant much to him.

As much as he enjoyed the Laurentians, he missed the sea – the wide open spaces and distant horizons – and so his annual journey to the Gaspé coast was very important to him.

Brandtner experimented extensively with various media and techniques. He decorated boxes, printed textiles, lino prints and woodcuts, worked on metal reliefs and wood carvings. These carvings show elements of Indian totem pole motifs, an influence from a visit to British Columbia in 1930. Such experiments led him close to the craft field, a move unacceptable to many of his contemporaries at a time when art and craft were rigidly separated.

A member of the Canadian Society of Painters in Water Colour, Brandtner served as its vice-president in 1945. He belonged to the Canadian Society of Graphic Art and the Canadian Group of Painters, acting as vice-president of the latter from 1944 to 1948 and in 1953. He was awarded the Jessie Dow prize for watercolour painting in 1946, first prize for painting in the Canadian Olympic contest in 1948, and in 1968/69, a Visual Arts Award from the Canada Council, Ottawa.

Brandtner participated in many exhibitions, among them a one-man show at the Picture Loan Society, Toronto, in 1938. His work was brought together with that of Louis Muhlstock in an exhibition of war industry drawings done at the Canadian Vickers' plant, Montreal, and shown at the National Gallery of Canada and the Art Gallery of Toronto in 1943. Another two-man show, this time shared with Léon Bellefleur, was exhibited at the Montreal Museum of Fine Arts in April 1950. Overseas, Brandtner was represented at the International Colour Woodcut Exhibition, Victoria and Albert Museum, London, in 1954.

Fritz Brandtner died November 7, 1969, in Montreal.

Fritz Brandtner

Art is a language through which the artist likes to express his feelings, emotions, reactions to the world surrounding him. I believe therefore, that art is not imitation of nature, and that I can only translate my vision, faith, rhythm, movement, tempo of this world into a new order, new unity, new forms, new spatial relationships, new balanced design. My paintings incorporate all the mentioned concepts and philosophies.

Fritz Brandtner, from his notebook.

18. Fritz Brandtner
Sixteen Islands, Laurentian Mountains, c. 1934/35
pastel and ink on paper
11½ x 14¼ in.   29.21 x 26.2 cm.

[2]Fritz Brandtner, from his notebook
[3]*Ibidem*

17. Fritz Brandtner
Laurel in the Laurentians, 1934
pastel and ink on paper
10 x 12½ in.   25.4 x 31.75 cm.

Maurice Cullen   1866-1934

Maurice Cullen was born in St. John's, Newfoundland, in 1866. His family settled in Montreal four years later.

He enjoyed drawing and clay modelling in his youth, and shortly after he was apprenticed to a dry goods merchant, his parents realized a mistake had been made. In 1886 they then let him enter the Monument National to study sculpture and drawing as a full time student.

A small legacy made it possible for him to continue his education in France. He was twenty-three when he entered the Beaux Arts de Paris, in the year of the acclaimed Claude Monet/Auguste Rodin exhibition.

Living in Paris at that time was very cheap, and life in the image of "la vie de bohème" changed the artistic direction of many North Americans. Maurice Cullen decided to abandon sculpture. His fine colour sense was stimulated by his new environment, by the work of the Impressionists and by the appreciation of painting nature. The Impressionists had moved art out of the studio and to outdoor scenes, colour and light patterns, atmospheric effects.

The Canadian artists Ludger Larose and Marc-Aurèle Suzor-Côté worked in the studio of painter Jules-Elie Delaunay (1828-1891). Maurice Cullen joined them. He had little patience with portrait painting and found the moods of his models irritating and distracting. Convinced that his talents lay in the direction of landscape painting, he travelled through provincial France, to Brittany and to Algiers. He also painted at Giverny, a small village seventy kilometers from Paris where the leader of

the Impressionist movement, Claude Monet, had established his residence. He had come to know the great master's son and it was a bitter disappointment to him not to be invited to visit the autocratic Monet's studio.

Monet's studies of light and its changing effect on nature, his need to paint subjects in series under different light conditions, influenced Cullen to carry out similar projects later on in life, especially during his years in the Laurentians. Though he did not adopt the divisionist technique of the early Impressionists, he believed strongly in keeping the colours as separate as possible to achieve the balance between vision and subject by means of a well-defined interplay of light and dark hues.

At twenty-eight, Maurice Cullen was elected an associate of the Société Nationale des Beaux Arts. His paintings were shown at the Salon exhibitions in Paris and the French Government bought his first winter landscape (painted in Brittany). A close friendship with the Montreal painter, James Wilson Morrice (one year older) had become important. However, late in 1895 he decided to return to Canada. Morrice joined him and they spent the winter painting around Beaupré on the North Shore of the St. Lawrence river. The following summer, they went together to Venice.

Twice more (1900 and 1902) Cullen returned to Europe, but his financial restrictions became acute. The public was not yet ready for the clean palette of the Impressionists.

Maurice Cullen's favourite seasons were early and late winter. He regarded the summer landscape, especially in the mountains, as "monotonous and too green," it did not appeal to him. He painted street scenes in Montreal, Quebec and environs, the icy shores of the river, the familiar views of the snowbound people living in a northern climate.

"One justification for living is the understanding and love of beauty," he said to his friend and dealer, William Watson.[1] To him, winter offered unlimited possibilities to express his identity with the silent world of gentle contrast.

In 1907 he became a full member of the Royal Academy. One year later the National Gallery of Canada purchased *First Snow* and his *Laurentian Landscape* was awarded the bronze medal at the International Exhibition at St. Louis, U.S.A.

Since success was slow in arriving, and, in order to "survive just one step ahead of the wolf,"[2] he undertook commissions for mural paintings in private homes – large decorative canvases which were quite distinct from his other works.

According to Robert Pilot, his stepson, he discovered Lac Tremblant in 1912 and from then on the Laurentians became the "…passionate love in his life. The lake, the mountains and the Caché River particularly, had an irresistible charm for him, and drew him back year after year, until the end of his life."[3]

After spending a physically and emotionally strenuous time near the front as a war artist in Europe, 1917/18, he built, in 1920, a painting cabin near Mont Tremblant, realizing his dream "to have a studio of my own, a shack in the mountains, an acre for a garden and every winter heavy with snow."[4]

For every large canvas he painted an original sketch, working in temperatures that made the patient application of oil paints extremely difficult. Occasionally he would carry an unfinished work to the place where he could complete it, crossing the deep snow on snowshoes.

In his studio he fabricated his own pastels from earth and other pigments in a wide range of tonalities. The formula for this old and most permanent medium had been given to him during his student days in Brittany by the American painter Fromuth.

Frustrated by the high cost of framing and dissatisfied with the ornateness of the current taste, for years he carefully carved his own frames, a vital part of his concept of the "artist craftsman."

From the early 1920s onwards he exhibited regularly and successfully. He was probably the only Canadian painter whose work would be sold out on the date of the opening at one-man exhibitions, even at the depth of the Depression years.

In 1930 the Government of Quebec held a retrospective of his work at the Ecole des Beaux-arts in Montreal. Another retrospective exhibition, arranged by the Art Gallery of Hamilton in 1956, was also shown at the Art Gallery of Ontario, the National Gallery of Canada and the Montreal Museum of Fine Arts.

Maurice Cullen died at his home in Chambly, Quebec, on March 28, 1934.

Maurice Cullen   On painting snow:
Snow colours reflect the tonalities of the sky and the sun. They turn blue, mauve, grey and even black but never into pure paper white. Pure white can therefore only be applied locally. Snow, like water, reflects the interplay and the changes of light in the atmosphere. But whereas a water surface may appear like a combination of countless tiny mirrors, snow shows fewer sides to light.

At dusk when the sun is warm and sits on the horizon, the snow appears red. The shadow of a cloud or a mountain also produces astonishing colours. When rivers come back to life in early spring, water rises above the ice and spreads slowly, contrasting in darkest blue, almost black, with the surrounding snow.

One has to look carefully and conscientiously and be patient.

La Revue Populaire, December 1927/28
Documentation Centre, Musée du Québec

21. Maurice Cullen
La Rivière du nord, 1932
oil on canvas
30¼ x 40 in.   76.8 x 101.6 cm.

[1]William R. Watson, *Retrospective, Recollections of a Montreal Art Dealer,* University of Toronto Press, 1974
[2]*Ibidem*
[3]From a speech made by Robert Pilot at the National Gallery of Canada, July 1948

[4]William R. Watson, *Retrospective, Recollections of a Montreal Art Dealer,* University of Toronto Press, 1974

22. Maurice Cullen

Evening on the Caché River, n.d.
pastel on paper
25 x 33 in. 63.5 x 83.82 cm.

Marc-Aurèle Fortin   1888-1970

Marc-Aurèle Fortin's familiarity with the Laurentians began in earliest childhood. He was one of fifteen children in his family, born March 15, 1888 in Ste Rose, then a village north of Montreal on the road to the mountains. The family lived in the city, but they had their second home in Ste Rose for weekends and holidays.

Fortin attended high school in Montreal. Early on he became interested in drawing, and studied it at the Ecole du Plateau with Ludger Larose and at the Monument National with Larose and Edmond Dyonnet between 1904 and 1907. At this time he also took courses in business administration and accountancy. His father, a lawyer, was decidedly against the idea of his son becoming an artist. Despite his mother's support and encouragement, father and son disagreed violently about the younger Fortin's future.

In the autumn of 1907, Fortin left Montreal for Edmonton where one of his brothers was living. He stayed there two years earning a living by working for the Post Office. He now began to paint seriously and, determined to further his education, he saved whatever he could towards studies at the highly reputed Art Institute of Chicago. Much of this time was spent in libraries, reading and researching, and this he continued to do through most of his life.

From Chicago he went to Boston and New York, mainly to visit the art galleries, museums and libraries. He returned to Montreal about 1912, and found accommodation in the *vieux quartier* of the city. Once again he worked for the Canadian Post Office.

The patriotic poetry of Albert Ferland (1872-1943) in praise of the Canadian soil and forests stimulated his pursuit of landscape subjects. Although he preferred to work in oil he had to accept the discipline of circumstances; watercolour lent itself better to quick outdoor sketching. These sketches, whose lack of intensity and depth frustrated his temperamental colour concept, served as reminders of a certain scene, and years later he would create a large painting from the earlier works.

From the early twenties, Fortin began showing his works to the public and was even able to sell some of them. His father, now a judge, was somewhat more reconciled to his son's unusual career and gave him a stipend which allowed Fortin to give up his job and devote himself to painting. His work now conveys a joyful expression of his newly-found freedom. The large canvases reflect the rich colours of the waterfront, the port, the city and lead to the *époque de grands arbres* as large trees began to dominate his works.

His interest in other techniques expanded the range of possibilities of expression: he experimented with etching, pastel, casein, using a variety of surfaces ranging from canvas to wood and even metal.

With money left to him on the death of his father in 1933, Fortin set out in 1934 for Europe, spending most of his time in Normandy, the south of France and northern Italy. He returned to Canada in 1935, and that same year a one-man exhibition of his works was held at the T. Eaton Co. Gallery, Montreal, where he was to exhibit on several occasions. In the following few years he tended to paint on black and grey backgrounds.

Fortin often depicted the region of Ste Rose, and also painted extensively in and around the Piedmont and Ste Adèle area of the Laurentians where he returned every autumn and sometimes during the spring months. He first discovered Charlevoix County in 1936, and from that year onwards he spent the early summer months either there or in the Gaspé region.

He bought himself a house in Ste Rose in 1949 and that same year he married, but this union did not last very long. Painting was his life and everything else, including his health, became a secondary concern. René Richard, the painter in Baie St Paul, in his moving recollection of his friend in 1970 described how Fortin was a gentle person, joyful in his work but unable to detach his thinking from painting for even a minute. He would return from outdoor sketching, spread his watercolour painting over the table and continue working on it rapidly with his pencil, emphasizing lines he remembered and outlining the rhythm of cloud formations.

Fortin suffered from ill-health most of his life and he stopped painting in 1955 due to this. That year one leg was amputated and the second four years later. He took up painting in the early sixties and from his wheelchair concentrated on works of large dimensions. But his poor health and inability to look after himself and his affairs eventually led him into penury and necessitated the sale of his house. In 1967 Fortin, old and almost blind, was taken to a hospital at Micamic, Abitibi, where he died in March 1970.

Fortin's works have been exhibited extensively: overseas in 1938, two of his works were chosen for inclusion in *A Century of Canadian Art* at the Tate Gallery, London, and in 1948 a one-man show was organized at the gallery of C. J. Van der A.A. at Almelo, Holland. But it is in his home province of Quebec that his paintings are best known. From 1942 until 1957, exhibitions of his work were shown every two years at the Galerie l'Art Français in Montreal. One-man exhibitions were held in the years that followed at the Musée du Québec in 1944; the Montreal Museum of Fine Arts in 1954 and in Montreal's Queen Elizabeth Hotel four years later. The National Gallery of Canada organized and circulated a retrospective exhibition, *Fortin*, in 1964; the Verdun Cultural Centre exhibited some 50 of his works from the collection of Mr. and Mrs. Jean Pierre Bonneville in 1968, and a short time after his death the Maison des Arts, Chicoutimi, held a retrospective exhibition sponsored by René Buisson. A major retrospective organized by Guy Robert was held at the Musée du Québec from December 9, 1976 to January 16, 1977.

Although Fortin was not nationalistic, his paintings have come to symbolize Quebec and the character of its countryside. They frequently contain elements of *art nouveau*, creating decorative patterns combined with bright colour and recurrently evoke a lively yet lyrical image of the Quebec landscape.

Marc-Aurèle Fortin

…but with nature one must be oneself. A painter must not stop at a few set formulas. He must always be progressing, looking for something better. The true artist never believes he has "arrived," he is constantly searching.

Marc-Aurèle Fortin; quoted in Jean Chauvin, *Ateliers*, Louis Carrier & Co., Monteal, 1928, p. 158.

26. Marc-Aurèle Fortin
Paysage, n.d.
oil on canvas
24 x 38¼ in.   61 x 97.1 cm.

Edwin Holgate   1892 –

Edwin Holgate was born on August 19, 1892 in Allendale, Ontario. His father, an engineer, moved his family to Jamaica three years later.

Young Edwin was sent back to Toronto to begin school, cared for by his uncle until his parents settled in Montreal in 1901.

Holgate was fourteen years old when he began to study in the Saturday class of William Brymner at the Art Association of Montreal. Five years later, after a summer class with Maurice Cullen at Beaupré, he became a full-time pupil of Brymner. His parents encouraged his setting out for Europe in

1912 to study at the Académie de la Grande Chaumière in Paris. There he developed his skill for spontaneous sketching.

With two friends he cycled from Paris to Naples, visiting art galleries and museums along the way, reading poetry, discussing Walter Pater's writings, art for art's sake, and the influence of the English Pre-Raphaelites. While in Paris, Edwin Holgate formed lasting friendships with Russian emigré artists and developed an interest in their cultural background. When, in July 1914, he travelled to the Ukraine with the bare minimum of luggage, he looked forward to a holiday with the families of his friends. The sudden outbreak of World War I left him stranded in Russia; his eventual return journey by Trans-Siberian Express east to Japan and from there to Victoria, B.C. took months.

Back in Montreal he joined the Canadian army. Posted overseas to Belgium and France, he was assigned to delivering ammunition along the defence lines. Painting was too difficult under the circumstances. Sketch books (which he carried either in his tunic pockets or tucked into the top of his boots) reveal the skill of a young artist in recording with compassion and spontaneity personal observations.

In 1919, demobilized, he settled briefly in Montreal and married his childhood friend Frances Rittenhouse the following year. Together they set out for Paris to continue their studies, Frances as a pianist and Edwin in the studio of the Russian expatriate artist Adolf Milman.

For the first time he could devote himself to what was to become a continuing interest – the chemistry of paint itself, the scientific study of pigments.

Edwin Holgate remembers vividly today how the students worked, stripped to the waist, churning and stirring the basic substance to produce all kinds of hues which would stimulate later experiments.

The technical knowledge and the insistance on craftsmanship Adolf Milman conveyed to his students made a lasting impression and set goals of excellence for the future.

At Concarneau, Brittany, the Holgates joined Robert Pilot. It was a summer of outdoor painting and sketching and youthful exuberance.

Edwin Holgate showed his work in his first one-man exhibition at the Montreal Arts Club shortly after his return to Canada in July 1922. He renewed his friendship with the group of dedicated artists who contributed much to the cultural development of Montreal – the Beaver Hall Group, which took its name from the square where they shared a studio in the early twenties.

In 1923 he built a cottage in the wilderness of the Mont Tremblant region of the Laurentians. Accessible only by boat, it offered him the privacy and surroundings he needed.

With A.Y. Jackson and folklorist Marius Barbeau he travelled to British Columbia in 1926 and painted in Indian communities along the Skeena River. The friendship with A.Y. Jackson was intimate. They went on many sketching trips in northern Ontario and down river to Murray Bay. Albert Robinson would join them and together they often visited Clarence Gagnon.

He enjoyed teaching at both the Ecole des Beaux-arts and the Art Association of Montreal, and at his own studio, where the distant sound of Frances' piano added to the informal atmosphere of more personal surroundings. Students, notably Jean Paul Lemieux, Stanley Cosgrove and Dr. Norman Bethune, became friends. Like his Paris tutor, Adolf Milman, he felt the need to share his technical experience and skill with young artists. Fluently bilingual, sensitive, an accomplished figure and landscape painter, he quietly established a position of influence.

He illustrated books and his woodcuts inspired other artists to use this technique.

In 1930 he was elected the eighth member of the Group of Seven, shortly before the Group held its last exhibition.

The duality of his life, at the refuge in the Laurentians and the income-producing work in the city, was interrupted from time to time by travel (to Labrador in 1932), by one-man exhibitions (1933, 1937), the creation of a décor for the Jasper Lounge in Ottawa's Château Laurier Hotel (1929), and a mural for the Canadian Pavilion at the New York World's Fair in 1939.

He was a Charter Member of the Canadian Group of Painters and elected in 1935 to full membership in the Royal Academy of Arts.

After the outbreak of World War II he set out for Halifax on his own to record in his sketchbook, as he did as a young man in Europe, the activity connected with war-time events. He was appointed Official War Artist with the R.C.A.F., 1943-44, and posted to England.

The Musée du Québec arranged a one-man exhibition in May 1944. The same year he decided to look for land, build a house and move to Morin Heights. In his words: "Like many others I was restless, exasperated, felt I'd go nuts if I didn't get away and try to find myself."[1]

Both he and Frances enjoyed the year-round country life. There was more time for painting – outdoors, mostly in small format, and the larger structured compositions on the easel in the studio. For several winters Edwin Holgate conducted Saturday morning art classes, held in various local halls. He became so much a part of the community that even today, three years after his return to Montreal, his presence in Morin Heights has not yet been quite accepted as a thing of the past. The move to the city had however become necessary for health reasons. This meant a painful break with casual country living.

Edwin Holgate's favourite motto "There is only one thing for an artist to do – paint!"[2] applies to his reluctance to give lectures, write articles on art or advocate publicly his own views.

In 1946 and 1970 he had one-man exhibitions at private galleries, and in 1953, an exhibition with Albert Cloutier at The Montreal Museum of Fine Arts.

The retrospective exhibition arranged for The National Gallery of Canada by Dennis Reid had to be kept small for travelling. It was shown in art galleries across Canada from July 1975 to June 1976, paying tribute not only to Edwin Holgate, the painter, but also to Edwin Holgate, the man who continued to go his own way, never asked for honours or sought them, and, who, acutely aware of the world around him, maintained his integrity above all else.

[1]Betty Shapiro, *The Gazette*, Montreal, August 10, 1963
[2]*Ibidem*

31. **Edwin Holgate**
Laurentian Cemetery, 1948
oil on panel
8½ x 10½ in.   21.6 x 26.7 cm.

32. **Edwin Holgate**
Laurentian Cemetery, 1949
oil on board
20⅛ x 24 in.   51.1 x 61 cm.

33. Edwin Holgate
Mountain Scene, 1929
oil on canvas
24 x 29 in.   60.96 x 73.66 cm.

45

Patrick Landsley   1926 –

Patrick Landsley was born in Winnipeg in 1926, the eldest of three children. His family lived on the outskirts of the city, the Prairies stretching beyond. He attended high school in Winnipeg, and from 1947 to 1949 studied at the Winnipeg School of Art under Lionel Lemoine FitzGerald and Joseph Plaskett, supporting himself by doing various jobs. Along with his fellow students at the school, Landsley had the opportunity to exhibit around town. Space was available to them in Eaton's department store and in the lobbies of theatres. The students were even able to sell some of their first works. At this time, he had little encouragement from his family about his desire to become an artist. His father hoped he would pursue a naval career.

During the late forties, Montreal appealed as the most lively centre of artistic life in Canada. Attracted by the number of well-known artists living there

at the time, Pat Landsley left home to enroll in The Montreal Museum of Fine Arts, School of Art and Design, in 1950. He studied there for two years, with Arthur Lismer, Jacques de Tonnancour and Goodridge Roberts. In 1952, he was awarded a Canada Foundation Scholarship for Overseas Study, and set out for Paris where he remained for a year.

He studied briefly with Fernand Léger at the Académie Montmartre. But he was uncomfortable in the ambience of this studio and felt unable to conform to Léger's method and approach to teaching art. A short time later, he enrolled at the Académie Ranson in Montparnasse where he studied drawing and painting with Gustave Singier, who became a firm friend as well as an influential teacher. Later, he acted as Singier's *massier,* hiring the model, organizing the studio and even acting as interpreter. The common language was English rather than French as many of the students who enrolled at the studio came from abroad.

Leaving Paris in 1953, Landsley stayed a few months in the Midlands, in England, where he printed butter wrappers in a factory in order to support himself while painting and earn enough for his return fare.

Back in Montreal in 1954, he was offered a teaching position at The Montreal Museum of Fine Arts, School of Art and Design, under Arthur Lismer. He accepted and remained there until 1966 giving classes in drawing and painting. He also taught at McGill University Department of Fine Arts from 1960 to 1967, and at the new University of Quebec in Montreal for two years, from 1970 to 1971. He began teaching at Concordia University in the Faculty of Fine Arts in 1966, and is now the Co-ordinator of its Drawing and Painting section.

Landsley's interest in the Laurentians began casually when he came to Montreal in the fifties. At that time he saw the paintings of Goodridge Roberts with whom he went on sketching trips to the Laurentians. But it was not until the early sixties that he became more involved with the landscape there. At first he had a cottage in the forest north of St Jovite, where he spent the summer months. Then, deciding that he wanted to settle more permanently in the Laurentians, but within reasonable distance of Montreal, he had a house designed by the architect Max Roth in the woods about eight miles from Ste Agathe. From then on he began to feel more and more at home with this landscape, more interested in the birds and plants that shared it with him, more intimate with the nature surrounding him. His painting has always been affected by nature – even in the mid-fifties when he belonged to the Association of Non-figurative Artists of Montreal, his work, although abstract, was nature-derived. Now, working in his windowed house that inspires him with the "sense of being inside and outside simultaneously," the landscape is a constant factor in his life. He does not work outside, or create paintings from on-the-spot sketches, preferring to rely on eyes and memory, draw on composites of visual experiences, and represent them as remembered. Space and light play an important role in these personal interpretations.

Landsley paints mainly in oil, but his more recent work combines acrylic with an overlay of oil paint. He used coloured ink in his early drawings, but now prefers pencil and colour pencil.

Driving the 70-odd miles to Concordia University in Montreal about twice a week is an interruption in his work as a painter, but Landsley enjoys the contact with other artists who are also teachers, and is stimulated by the teaching itself.

He has exhibited in various group exhibitions across Canada, and in several one-man and two-man shows, particularly in Montreal and Winnipeg. He was resident artist at the Saidye Bronfman Art Centre, Montreal, 1974–1975.

Patrick Landsley
Since 1968 I have lived up in the Laurentians. The house, in which there are large areas of glass, has had a strong effect on my recent painting – the winter landscape of the Laurentians – the sense of being inside and outside simultaneously, the recurrence of the window motif. The landscape is constantly changing from season to season and also due to the time of day. I often leave when the moon and the stars are still out and these symbols occur in my work. The special light that is here is a strong influence, in the same way that the light was special in Brittany and in the south of France for the painters who lived there and were conscious of this quality.

Patrick Landsley
October 1976

35. Patrick Landsley
Winter Eclipse, 1975

coloured pencil, charcoal and pencil on paper
11½ x 12½ in. 29.21 x 31.75 cm.

John Lyman   1886 – 1967

John Lyman was born in 1886 in Biddeford, Maine, at the home of his maternal grandfather. His American father, a naturalized Canadian, established the family residence in Montreal the same year.

John Lyman grew up in Montreal. At the age of fourteen he went with his father to the Mediterranean, the Middle East and Paris before entering Hotchkiss, a preparatory school in Connecticut where he stayed until the start of his writing studies at McGill University in Montreal. He believed in the possibility of a journalistic career and only gradually developed an interest in painting.

In the spring of 1907 he returned to Paris, spending the summer in the atelier of Marcel Béronneau. This teacher's method of stimulating the concentrated rapid approach to sketching, the quick assessing of essential forms free of superfluous detail, was to have a lasting influence on John Lyman's later work.

He went to Brittany to paint landscapes. His mind was made up to become an artist, to remain in Europe. After a brief attempt at studying architectural design at the Royal College of Art in London he enrolled at the studio of Jean-Paul Laurens at the Académie Julien in Paris. It was a bitter experience, a vain attempt to conform to an academic style which some of the students still tried to perfect after ten or fifteen years of studying.

He met another young expatriate from Montreal, James Wilson Morrice, and Matthew Smith, the English painter, both accomplished artists. He was introduced to Gertrude Stein and at her weekly salon, surrounded by a growing collection of modern art, his artistic goals became more ambitious. He decided in the autumn of 1909 to study at the informal Académie Matisse. Six months later he fell seriously ill and this marked the end of his student years.

In April 1911 he married Corinne Saint-Pierre in Montreal, returned to France, painted and travelled, assiduously developing his own style. Two years later his work was roundly rejected by hostile critics in Montreal. Four paintings at the Spring Exhibition and his first one-man show made him the target for ridicule in a city which still ignored the by now important Fauve movement in Europe.

When the war broke out he failed a medical examination for the Canadian Army and with his wife Corinne joined the Red Cross. They were each awarded the Médaille de la Reconnaissance Française for distinguished services.

The winter of 1918-1919 was spent in Los Angeles, but for the next twenty years the Lymans lived abroad – Paris, Cagnes-sur-Mer, Spain, North Africa and Bermuda.

John Lyman's paintings were accepted by the Salons in Paris and exhibited in company with the works of his contemporaries Derain, Utrillo, Dufy, Matisse and Vlaminck. In October 1927 his second one-man show in Montreal was well received. A third exhibition took place shortly before the Lymans' return to Montreal in early spring, 1931. The influence of contemporary Paris had been slow in reaching the city. Now the climate was right for promotion of the new concepts in art and the independent art trends expressed by young and talented Canadians.

John Lyman established with André Biéler and others the "Atelier," based on the principle of the Académie Julien – offering some guidelines but most of all studio space, a model and the opportunity to discuss problems with a master.

Subsequent exhibitions at Henry Morgan Galleries by the Atelier group included work by John Lyman, André Biéler, Edwin Holgate, Marc-Aurèle Fortin and Goodridge Roberts.

The Lymans' country home in St Jovite became the gathering place for artists and, in the early thirties, the site of a summer art school established with the assistance of Harold Beament.

In 1939 John Lyman formed the Eastern Group with six other painters. In the same year he was a key figure in the founding of the Contemporary Art Society, for which he served as president for six years. Through this society which brought artists and lay members together, he stimulated annual exhibitions of contemporary French art.

His monthly column in *The Montrealer* contributed to the evolution of the arts in the province of Quebec. These articles, always topical and relating to every aspect of the visual arts, reveal the knowledge and courage of the writer he had hoped to become when at the age of seventeen he wrote to his father (March 29, 1903): "I believe in a literary destination and to rise to a position which would enable me to revolutionize modern periodical literature." His own painting came closer to the concept Henri Matisse expressed in 1908 in *Notes d'un Peintre*: "What I dream of is an art of balance, purity and serenity, devoid of troubling or depressing subject matter…."

In 1948 Lyman was appointed Associate Professor of the Department of Fine Arts at McGill University; 1951 Professor and Chairman of the same. In 1953 he was honoured with a Fellowship by the Royal Society of Arts in London.

John Lyman's work was exhibited in the United States, Britain, South America and France, including the Tate Gallery in London and the National Gallery in Washington.

He had liked to think of himself in the imagery of Robert Frost, whom he quoted in a diary entry for October, 1950:

> *I took the road less travelled by*
> *And that has made all the difference.*
I have never followed the fashion in painting but rather recoiled from it. I have never cultivated a manner, that mimickry of style. This is why although when I was young I was thought scandalously 'modern', today I am generally called a conservative and even sometimes taken for an academic by those for whom 'modernism' means nothing but popular patterns of abstraction or neo-primitivism.

On the occasion of his 80th birthday in 1966, a collection of 148 oils and 46 watercolours and drawings was shown first at the Musée du Québec, and later at Montreal's Musée d'Art contemporain.

A few months later, following a lengthy illness, he died in Barbados.

John Lyman
I am not sure that I like a studio with a view. When I have seen something, I like to go indoors and dream about it, evoke it and formulate it. An ever changing expanse outside the window keeps intruding and I see so many things that finally I see nothing. No, a studio should not have more than a limited and very familiar view.

John Lyman Diary, Volume II
Bibliothèque Nationale du Québec, Montreal
Handwritten text, date of entry: July 1957

37. John Lyman
St Jovite, n.d.
watercolour on paper
9³/₈ x 11⁷/₈ in.   46.99 x 30.16 cm. (sight)

36. John Lyman
Oat Field in the Laurentians, 1942
oil on wood
14¹⁵/₁₆ x 18¹/₈ in.   38 x 46 cm.

38. John Lyman

Haying by the Lake, n.d.
oil on canvas
18 x 22 in. 45.7 x 55.8 cm.

photo: Gabor Szilasi, 1976

Louis Muhlstock   1904 –

Louis Muhlstock's family came to Canada from
Eastern Europe in the early part of this century. He
was born in 1904 in Narajow, Galicia, which is now
Poland but was then part of the Austro-Hungarian
Empire. The empire was in its last years of decline
and disintegration, leading to its final destruction
in the First World War.

For a poor Jewish family, life in Galicia was marked
by hardship and oppression. Rival nationalisms
fought among themselves and with the waning
imperial authority. In 1908, the imperial *statthalter*
(governor) was assassinated for his pro-Russian views
by a Ukrainophile student. That same year Louis'
father, a trader who found he could not make a
living, left for Montreal.

It was two years before he could gain a foothold as
a fruit dealer and send for the rest of the family.
Louis, with his mother, two brothers and a sister,
arrived in Canada in 1911. The family moved into a
basement flat on St Dominique Street, off "The
Main" (St Lawrence Boulevard), a noisy, lively
district in Montreal's east end.

Political upheaval and social tension build strong
family loyalties and determination. The Muhlstocks
needed these qualities in Montreal, then a city of
the very rich and the very poor. Father Muhlstock,
an avid reader of the Talmud, instilled in his children
the importance of learning. They did not, like most
of their friends, leave school early to earn a living.
"We too worked hard, but without neglecting our
studies,"[1] Louis recalls. He also remembers the sheer
joy when, after twelve years of living in a dark home,
they moved to the sunny side of the street and to a

[1] Monique Saumier, *Louis Muhlstock: un démi-siècle de
peinture,* Thesis, Concordia University, Montreal,
1975

52

higher floor flooded with sunlight.

In 1918 Muhlstock enrolled at the Monument National. He had been sketching ever since he learned how to hold a pencil. Impatient to follow evening classes after school, he pretended to be two years older in order to gain admission.

For the next ten years he spent his free time at art schools from the Monument National to the Royal Academy, courses at the Art Association and, 1926/27, at the Ecole des Beaux-arts. After finishing his secondary school education, he worked as an accountant in an import firm, living frugally, saving every penny he could in order to realize his dream to study in Europe.

In the autumn of 1928 he set out for Paris and immediately registered at the Académie de la Grande Chaumière. For three years he did mostly figurative studies. His principal teacher, Louis François Biloul, though not an innovative painter himself, was nevertheless capable of giving Muhlstock the training he needed. In the second year his appointment as *massier* – responsible for arranging the classes and timing the poses of the models – relieved the financial burden of paying the daily five franc fee.

During vacation time he painted outdoors in the country, in Brittany and the Jura mountains near the Swiss border, and he went to Belgium and England to visit museums.

In 1931 this period came to an abrupt end. He rushed home to Montreal to be near his seriously ill mother. "For many years I kept my return ticket," Louis recalls, "but by now the Depression had spread and there was no way to raise money for living again in Europe."[2]

[2]Louis Muhlstock, interview with Lawrence Sabbath, *Canadian Art*, July 1960

Poverty and unemployment, the stark realities of his environment, began to influence his thinking and his work. Deeply moved by the plight of the poor and the underprivileged, and by people sitting patiently in hospital waiting rooms and, during the war, by factory and shipyard workers, he revealed in every line of his drawings his intense compassion and respect for human dignity.

The sharing of an experience beyond pure visual appearance, the love for transmitting his own beliefs and joys of discovery in the human figure extended into other areas – still life, street scenes, interiors, animals, trees and plants. It extended into close friendships with other painters and writers. Hector de Saint-Denys Garneau and Miriam Waddington dedicated poems; the composer Murray Adaskin, in his *In Praise of Canadian Painting in the Thirties* for strings and harpsichord, entitled the Adagio movement, *Louis Muhlstock*. Commissioned by the Chamber Players of Toronto through a grant from the Canada Council it was performed by the Chamber Players in Toronto on January 24, 1976.

"The painter's job," Louis asserts, "does not end when the work of art is produced." This "job" and the need to communicate through human relationships led to active participation in the Contemporary Art Society, of which he was a founding member in 1949; the Kingston Conference, 1941 and the Canadian Group of Painters, 1942; and to personal support through donation of works to numerous causes, local as well as international. He also was elected member of the Canadian Society of Graphic Arts and the Canadian Society of Painters in Water Colour.

After his return from Europe he went back to the Laurentians, which he had explored often in his youth. Now, in the 1930s he sketched and painted in

the regions around Mont Rolland, Piedmont, Val Morin and Ste Agathe, mostly in the autumn, staying at guest houses where, he recalls, room and board for a week would cost eight dollars.

In 1947 the Muhlstock family bought "une terre," 140 acres of farmland in Val David, with a rural home and barns.

Muhlstock never took his discoveries for granted: the movement of the farm animals, the rich variety of textures in the forest, the tonalities of the hillsides changing through the seasons. He paints and sketches outdoors even in the bitter cold. He also feels that there is no particular distinction between his life in the city and up at the farm, no conscious need to "escape" from either environment.

Louis Muhlstock has exhibited regularly in both public and private galleries. He participated first, with two portrait studies, at the Montreal Spring Exhibition in 1925 and in 1930–1931 at the Salon des Artistes Français in Paris. From then on his works were included in many important Canadian exhibitions circulated nationally and abroad, as well as international exhibitions.

Frequent one-man shows were held in Montreal, notably at the Art Association, 1933, 1940, 1942, 1948; The Montreal Museum of Fine Arts, 1952, 1959; the Verdun Cultural Centre, 1972; in Toronto with the Picture Loan Society, 1937, 1938; the Art Gallery of Toronto and also at Hart House, University of Toronto, 1939. In 1967 he was awarded the Canada Centenary Medal.

His recent retrospective exhibition, *A Survey of Forty-Five Years* was arranged by the Art Gallery of Windsor in 1976.

40. Louis Muhlstock
Laurentian Boulders, 1973
brown (sepia) chalk (slight wash) on paper
20 x 26 in.   50.8 x 66.04 cm.

41. Louis Muhlstock
Autumn (Isola) Val David, Laurentians, 1975
oil on canvas board
16 x 20 in. 40.64 x 50.8 cm.

Roland Pichet   1936 -

Roland Pichet was a child of Montreal's east end. He was born on July 4, 1936, his mother of Irish descent and his father French-Canadian. After dropping out of high school, Pichet earned a living at odd jobs while he studied drawing, painting and sculpture in night school at the Ecole des Beaux-arts. While at the Beaux-arts, from 1955 to 1959, he and several of his friends took drawing lessons from the Catalonian artist Alfredo Monros.

In 1960, Pichet met the outstanding artist Albert Dumouchel and enrolled in his print-making course at the Beaux-arts. Dumouchel had a strong influence on his growth as an artist and on his work. In 1962 Pichet won first prize in a provincially sponsored graphics contest. That same year he was invited to teach as Dumouchel's assistant, on the recommendation of Jacques de Tonnancour and Jean Simard.

Pichet obtained his first Canada Council grant in 1963 which enabled him to set off for Paris in the spring of 1964. There he studied at the Atélier de Lithographie Desjobert et Jean Pons, with these two master printers. He also spent a brief period in England and Holland. At this time his friend, writer Guy Robert, invited him to collaborate on a lithography series illustrating the poem *L'Eau et La Pierre*. This, for Pichet, was just the beginning of a continuing passion for *La Grande Edition*, series of prints complementing poems and presented in luxury portfolios.

Returning to Montreal, Pichet prepared for his first one-man exhibition of paintings at the Galerie Libre, Montreal, in 1966. The following year he decided to leave Montreal for London, where, with further assistance from the Canada Council, he was able to work steadily for a year, continuing research and experimentation into various aspects of print-making, using the facilities of the Slade School of Art.

Stimulated by the company of many congenial people and the influential trends of British art in the sixties, he pursued his investigation of pure colour contrast from the print series *Tick-Tocker* to large format painting on canvas. His discovery of acrylic paint as a medium led him into the field of linear rhythm composition which was at first hard-edge with sharp colours, and then became softer, more natural, moving towards the present horizontal lyricism in his landscapes.

Pichet went back to work at the Ecole des Beaux-arts on his return to Montreal. In 1969, the school was incorporated with the University of Quebec where from September of that year until the present time, Pichet has been head of the printmaking department. He sometimes found the administrative side of the job exhausting, causing him at one time to give up painting for more than a year.

In May 1971, Roland and his wife Suzanne moved from Montreal to Piedmont. The Laurentians were familiar. As a child he had listened as his grandfather, a logger, told the stories of *les hommes du nord*, their logging exploits on the Rouge and the North Rivers, their return to St Jérome from the lumber camps, and of the forest north of the city where these men passed so much of their lives. Later, at a summer camp near Lac Tamarcouta, and on sketching trips around Morin Heights, he came to know the Laurentians for himself. As a student he spent much of his time there, particularly during the winter months, with friends from the Beaux-arts.

Soon after the move to Piedmont, Pichet completed a series of twenty-five watercolours and fifteen acrylics which he called *Suite Laurentienne*. These made up an exhibition which was held at the Apogée Art Gallery in St Sauveur-des-Monts in August 1971. Pichet exhibited here in St Sauveur annually from 1969 to 1975. Since 1960 to the present, Pichet's work has been included in various group exhibitions, in Canada and abroad; he had a one-man show at the Richard Demarco Gallery, Edinburgh in 1968 and a two-man show, shared with Mel Boyaner at the Gallery Pascal, Toronto, in 1970.

Pichet combines teaching with his own painting. He works in a studio surrounded by the trees of the Laurentian forest. An enthusiastic hunter and cross-country skier, he explores the countryside during the fall and winter seasons, taking photographs as a reminder of certain places he wants to record, and drawing on his visual memory to interpret the landscape. He continues to make limited editions of fine serigraphs, often to accompany texts or poems by Quebec writers which express the spirit and feeling of Quebec and its countryside, his images reflecting the same sentiment.

Roland Pichet

Since I have been working here, I have found a new dimension to life and to my work. I always await winter impatiently: the snowy silence with its different hues of white and the interplay of the greys; the white fields reaching towards distant hills, marked by fence posts, snow fences and all sorts of stalks and twigs. Days of extreme cold in January, almost like those of Provence in their luminosity, bring on the dream of other places. I would like to travel more through Quebec, especially during the winter, to remote northern regions inhabited by Indians and Inuit. This country which to me looks essentially linear has to be seen and explored and one has to live in it to understand its magic.

Pichet
18 October 1976

photo: Basil Zarov, 1976

43. b Roland Pichet
Suite Québecoise: blues pour un piquet de clôture, 1975
serigraph
13 x 20 in.   33.02 x 50.8 cm.

43.c Roland Pichet

Suite Québecoise: blues pour un piquet de clôture, 1975
serigraph
13 x 20 in.   33.02 x 50.8 cm.

Robert Wakeham Pilot   1898-1967

Robert Pilot was a Newfoundlander, born October 9, 1898 in St. John's. His father died when he was still a child. In 1910 his mother remarried and Maurice Cullen, also a Newfoundlander, became Pilot's stepfather; the family moved to Montreal in 1911.

Pilot grew up in the environment of an artist's studio, learned the techniques of painting and drawing from Cullen and went to evening classes at the Monument National. The year 1915 was specially important for him as he began studying with William Brymner at the Art Association of Montreal. Pilot did not have enough money for the fees but Brymner encouraged him to start immediately and pay later. His artistic career was interrupted in March 1916 when he enlisted with the Fifth Division Artillery and served overseas for three years. In January 1919 he returned to Montreal and to the Art Association. That same year he won the Wood Scholarship.

Soon afterwards, Pilot returned to France for the next three years. He enrolled at the Académie Julien in Paris, studying with Jean-Pierre Laurens, an artist whom he admired. He spent the summer of 1921 in Concarneau, Brittany and returned there again the following summer where he was joined by Edwin Holgate and his wife Frances. They, like Pilot, had left Montreal for France in 1920. Holgate shared Pilot's studio for a few months.

Pilot's appreciation and love of the country had early on been nurtured by the sketching trips that he had undertaken in his youth with Cullen. Returning to Montreal, he used his stepfather's former studio on Ste Famille Street as his base, and from there made various excursions. He said of that time:
I had the definite idea of what I wished to do and that was to interpret the Canadian scene, particularly the Province of Quebec and, more especially, the city and environs of Quebec.[1]
This was to become one of his main achievements, though he also made sketching trips to the Maritimes and returned to Europe again several times; notably he made a number of sketches of Spain and Morocco in 1927. He was familiar with many areas of the Laurentians where he spent much time over the years, particularly around the North River at Mont Rolland and Piedmont, St Sauveur, Val Morin, St Jovite, Lac Supérieur and the adjacent Devil River, and the country surrounding Mont Tremblant.

Robert Pilot was mainly a painter of landscapes. He worked as much as he could *en plein air* and would often take one canvas seven or eight times to the same spot:
And then you're up against the weather, you have to pick the same time of the day, the colouring and such, and it's rather hazardous in the sense that you're at the mercy of the elements.[2]

At times this led him to set up his easel in his jeep, and paint while looking through the three rear windows; he said it worked almost perfectly, even with a 21″ x 28″ canvas. He worked in his studio only to escape the inclement winter weather, and he would sometimes have several canvases in the making simultaneously.

He favoured oil painting over other media. Although he experimented in preparing his own canvases, he preferred to use prepared canvas, and bought the best art materials available. He made a limited number of fine etchings, mostly of Quebec City and its surroundings.

Pilot's painting has been regarded as derivative from that of his stepfather, Maurice Cullen. He himself was aware of this influence so close to him, but he was also deeply conscious of the consequences that it could impose on his work, particularly that undertaken in the Laurentians. In a letter to a friend from the Piedmont Hotel, Laurentian Mountains, he wrote:
I feel a little more satisfied with the material I'll have to work on as yesterday & today I found two excellent motifs which I hope to make something of. The country here – the formations of the hills particularly – is really fine. I find it hard to keep M.C. out of my mind but I'm beginning to discover that I will be able to do the Laurentians after all in my own way (otherwise I'd give them up). I see things again and again that haven't been "done"...[3]
He went on to add that there is "still not a soul in the hotel" despite the boast on its letterhead of "First Class Board" and "The best Ski-ing place in the Laurentians."

Pilot was a strong supporter of the Royal Canadian Academy and considered it a beneficial force for artists and art in Canada. He was an Associate as early as 1925 and elected to full membership in

[1]Robert Pilot, interviewed by Lawrence Sabbath, *Canadian Art*, Sept./Oct. 1961
[2]*Ibidem*
[3]Letter to a friend, March 22, 1935

1934. He served as President in 1953-54. The Jessie Dow prize was given to Pilot twice, in 1932 and 1934.

With the outbreak of World War II, Pilot felt he could not stand aside. He volunteered and served as officer in the Black Watch (Royal Highland Regiment) of Canada in Europe from 1940 to 1945. He was awarded the M.B.E. in 1944. In Italy, he revisited places and museums that had meant much to him.

Robert Pilot's works were exhibited at the Watson Art Galleries, Montreal, where he had one-man shows during the twenties, thirties and forties. He was a regular exhibitor at the shows of the Royal Canadian Academy, and other exhibitions of particular note include a retrospective of some thirty-five works at the Kitchener-Waterloo Art Gallery in March 1967. A major retrospective organized by The Montreal Museum of Fine Arts, co-ordinated by T.R. MacDonald, then director of the Art Gallery of Hamilton, was exhibited at these two galleries as well as The National Gallery of Canada, from November 1968 to February 1969.

Throughout his life, Pilot read extensively – literature, philosophy, the history of art. Books were a very vital part of his life.

He died in Montreal in December 1967 after a lengthy illness.

Robert Pilot
I firmly believe the only way to get anything new in painting is to keep on working sincerely in front of nature and one good day a secret will be revealed to you. The age of impatience hurts painting. The old days of candlelight and reflection seem to be gone and a consequent loss of something from within coming out.

Letter to a friend, November 21, 1927

46. Robert Pilot
Lac Supérieur, P.Q., c. 1946
oil on canvas
21½ x 27½ in.   54.61 x 69.85 cm.

photo: Basil Zarov, 1976

Jean-Paul Riopelle   1923 –

Jean-Paul Riopelle was born on October 7, 1923, in Montreal. He grew up in the east end of the city. His father was a builder/architect and Jean-Paul was an only child, whose ability and interest in drawing were recognized at an early age. From the age of six onward he studied on weekends with a tutor, Henri Bisson, a Montreal sculptor and painter who although opinionated (he did not approve of the Impressionists) encouraged the curiosity and inventiveness of his pupil. They regularly went sketching in the Laurentians, observing and recording nature. In winter they shared a studio, respecting each other's privacy and activity.

Childhood holidays were spent in the Laurentians, the Gaspé, other parts of Quebec and in the Thunder Bay region of Ontario. It was at Fort William, for lack of summer companions, that the young Jean-Paul realized for the first time the importance of becoming bilingual.

At fifteen, during a summer holiday in Gaspé, Riopelle worked on a sketch of seaweeds and sand as seen through the glittering surface of water. He tried and succeeded in rendering a realistic impression of what he observed. At the same time the magic of abstraction and its possibilities became apparent to him. From then on in his development, figurative studies and landscape compositions lost their meaning. His experiments led him strongly into the direction of the prismatic approach to forms and patterns in nature, reflecting his temperament and his capacity for trusting his memory of the essence of things seen.

Along with his interest in art, Riopelle had and still has a facility for mathematics. For two years he studied engineering at the Polytechnical Institute, and took evening classes at the Ecole des Beaux-arts.

He was nineteen when the Annual Spring Exhibition at The Museum of Fine Arts in Montreal accepted his first entry, a luminous impression of a distant city.

During the war years, many of the greatest European paintings were sent to Canada for safekeeping. Some of these treasures were exhibited in Montreal. Riopelle went back again and again to study them: Tintoretto, El Greco, van Gogh – what fascinated him in the paintings was not so much the pictorial content but the techniques, the *métier.*

He was twenty years old when he decided to abandon engineering and to study art with Paul-Emile Borduas, Maurice Gagnon and Marcel Parizeau at the Ecole du Meuble. Borduas, a mature and disciplined master, encouraged free expression in the work of his students. From the talented and dedicated ones he expected results.

Riopelle became part of the nucleus of the group which was later to be known as "Les Automatistes," (a name which some of the artists resented because it did not apply to the nature of their work), the supporters of the most courageous revolutionary statement ever made in the history of Quebec art, the "Refus Global." The range of interests shared by the group was extensive and reached into many directions of creative contemporary thinking and links with the surrealist movements in other countries.

In 1945 Riopelle shared a studio with Marcel Barbeau and the poet Rémi-Paul Forgues, later with Jean-Paul Mousseau and Fernand Leduc. The radical cultural movement gained strength. Group exhibitions in Montreal and in New York (1946) followed. But Riopelle, though participating in the shows, had left in January the same year for Paris, after a brief stay in New York.

He worked, in New York, for a window display firm creating objects in *papier mâché.* Post-war France was not yet ready to welcome foreigners for unlimited periods and purposes. Riopelle was granted a visa and residence permit as sole agent for a taximeter firm. He took his duties quite seriously, the basic technical skills acquired at the Polytechnical came in use and he became an expert, respected by the garage mechanics, in the repair problems of the Paris taximeter system.

Fernand Leduc joined him in March 1947 and the two arranged an exhibition for their Montreal group "Les Automatistes" in June at the Galérie du Luxembourg. The day after the opening Riopelle signed the "Ruptures inaugurales," the international Surrealist manifesto. In July his work was included in the Exposition Internationale du Surréalisme organized by André Breton and Marcel Duchamp at the Galerie Maeght in Paris.

He travelled extensively in Europe and decided to settle in Paris. In the late 1940s he took a new interest in sculpture, a form which had always attracted him. Though the clay models of this early period broke, they were, according to Riopelle, similar to the snowsculptures of his youth and the sculpture he creates now in large format.

From 1949 onwards his one-man exhibitions have been yearly events in important private and public galleries on both sides of the Atlantic. He was granted a Canadian Government Fellowship in 1953; a Doctorate of Letters at McGill University in 1968 and a Doctorate of Laws by the University of Manitoba in 1972.

In 1962 he was awarded the Prix UNESCO at the Biennale in Venice. Retrospective exhibitions in Canada include: 1963, The National Gallery of Canada (also shown at the Art Gallery of Ontario and The Montreal Museum of Fine Arts); 1967, Musée du Québec; October 1976, Place des Arts, Montreal; from June 15 to October 12, 1972, the Centre culturel canadien and the Musée d'Art moderne de la ville de Paris honoured him with one-man exhibitions in a joint venture.

Riopelle works in different media and sizes: painting in oil, acrylic, gouache, watercolour; *assemblage,* etching, lithography; drawing in inks, charcoal, sanguine (red chalk); and sculpture. His intricate charcoal/sanguine drawings were woven, in *haute lisse,* by the Manufacture des Gobelins into the two tapestries representing Canada at the 4th and 5th Biennial of Tapestry in Lausanne, Switzerland. These works are now in the collection of Le Mobilier National, Paris.

The major themes of Riopelle's work are always related to nature. The *Hibou* (Owl) series as well as the *Ficelles et autres Jeux* (based on Inuit string games), the Forest and Trees, Panorama and Horizon paintings reflect the intimate inner identity of the man with his natural environment; in the words of author Paul Auster: "Jean-Paul Riopelle is a man who knows the forest, and his paintings are an expression of this search for the thing-in-itself. The almost limitless energy we find in his canvases does not speak of an abstract program to become one-with-nature, but of a tangible need to be present, to be here, to see the thing that is."[1]

[1]Paul Auster, Introduction to Pierre Matisse Exhibition Catalogue, 1975

Since 1974 his studio at Lac Masson, in the Laurentians, allows him to combine his frequent visits to Canada with the continuity of his work and a closer contact with a countryside he has always loved. He maintains a painting studio in St Cyr near Paris and shares with the Spanish artist Miró a sculpture studio at St Paul de Vence in southern France.

His home is at Vétheuil, France, on the property owned formerly by Claude Monet, the French Impressionist painter.

Though he has many close friendships with writers and artists, Riopelle remains an intensely private person, avoiding interviews and public appearances, leaving it to others to explain his beliefs and the underlying message of his work.

In 1976 he returned with a new intensity to drawing in large format (coloured ink, charcoal/sanguine) extending, by joining the sheets of paper, the compositions to almost mural size. They may lead into a new media – glass – and a yet further inquiry into the possibility of reaching behind the mirror, which he attempted in his print series *Derrière le Miroir* ten years ago.

Jean-Paul Riopelle
I see everything I create as part of what I see, what I have seen in the past, yesterday or years ago when I was a child – close to the earth. For me, everything is landscape.

Jean-Paul Riopelle in conversation with Helen Duffy, July 30, 1976

48. Jean-Paul Riopelle
Untitled, 1976
ink on paper
21½ x 26 in. 54.6 x 66 cm.

49. *Untitled*, 1976
ink on paper
26 x 21½ in. 66 x 54.6 cm.

50. *Untitled*, 1976
ink on paper
21½ x 26 in. 54.6 x 66 cm.

51. *Untitled*, 1976
ink on paper
21½ x 26 in. 54.6 x 66 cm.

Summer 1961

Goodridge Roberts   1904-1974

Goodridge Roberts came from New Brunswick, though he was born in Barbados, where his parents were living temporarily. He spent his early childhood in Fredericton and at the age of six moved with his family to England and France for two years, after which they returned to Fredericton.

His father, Theodore Goodridge Roberts, poet and novelist, was already in the reserve army when the war broke out in 1914. He was posted to active duty overseas immediately and his wife and children followed him to England. The family remained there until 1919.

Goodridge Roberts started to draw and paint during those years. All his life he remembered the moment of first awareness of light and colour that came to

him as a child, walking through a London park in sunshine after rain. "Soon afterward," he recalled many years later, "I went into Kensington Gardens with some watercolours and a pad and painted some trees by the Serpentine."[1]

During his high school years in Fredericton he became interested in reading and writing poetry, while he continued with painting. In 1923 he entered the newly opened Ecole des Beaux-arts in Montreal where, during his first year, he won all the prizes. During the second year, when he developed a style of his own, he won none at all.

When he was twenty-two, he studied at the Art Students' League, New York, with John Sloan, Max Weber and Boardman Robinson. Here for the first time he saw original work of Cézanne, Picasso and

Matisse and was introduced to the world of the Italian Primitives and Giotto. He painted still lifes and figures and made quick sketches of people – humourous drawings as well as figure drawing with longer poses.

He returned to Fredericton in 1929 to work as a draftsman with the provincial forestry service. But he continued to paint steadily, setting himself the task of doing one watercolour before work each morning and another one in the evening.

When he was twenty-six Roberts moved to Ottawa. Though he had not yet exhibited in public, he organized a class at the Ottawa Art Association and opened a summer school for painting at Wakefield, Quebec. His participation in group shows at the Ottawa Art Association was followed by his first one-man exhibition at the Arts Club in Montreal. Then in September 1933, Roberts became the first resident artist at Queen's University in Kingston, Ontario, on a grant provided by the Carnegie Foundation.

Roberts' first stay in the Laurentians north of Montreal in 1937, at Morin Heights, was to be followed by many summers in the area: 1939 and 1940 (at John Lyman's farm house) near St Jovite; 1941 and 1942, St Alphonse; 1946, Piedmont; 1949, Fourteen Island Lake; 1950, Weir; 1953, near Morin Heights; and 1954, Montfort.

Goodridge Roberts liked both rugged and pastoral summer countryside. He worked in the Gatineau Hills of Ottawa, the Eastern Townships of Montreal, the Lower St. Lawrence region, Georgian Bay, Cape Breton Island, and on a brief trip through the Gaspé. He painted near St Raphael on the Côte d'Azur, while on a Canadian Government Overseas

[1]Goodridge Roberts, "From this point I looked out," *Queen's Quarterly*, Autumn 1953

Fellowship for one year of work and study in France during 1953/54. Invited by the editors of *Canadian Art* to express his feelings about this period, he wrote:

It might be assumed that because I am a painter and because I went abroad for the purpose of looking at works of art that these works of art as such, removed from external associations, would have been what most affected me. However I don't know that this is the case in spite of the profound pleasure I had from many of these and the conviction I felt that they were expressions of deep understanding.

Perhaps rather than any revelation of a pictorial nature, I am conscious of having come to a fuller awareness, through my extended stay in Paris and my limited travels in a few European countries, of such wider implications as art's close identification with history, the shortness of the individual's life and the deathlessness of man's spirit.

Studying, as I did during that year, what men had built and painted and carved during so many centuries and seeing these works in countries still disfigured and impoverished by recent wars, I had brought home to me very forcibly how this process of building up and destroying had always been going on and that in every great work of art an awareness of this need both to create and to kill is evident.

In looking at these profound proofs of some men's understanding of humanity, whether through the humble jugs and loaves of Chardin, the courage and serenity of Rembrandt, Michelangelo's tormented grandeur, the swagger and tragedy of Picasso, the joyful well-being of Renoir or the troubled fervour of van Gogh, I felt conscious, through these men's pictures, of the universality and ever-presence of such feelings and that, as there always has been, there always must continue to be this transmutation of man's spirit into forms of art.[2]

From 1938 onwards his work was exhibited regularly in private and public galleries in Canada, the United States and overseas, notably with touring exhibitions arranged by The National Gallery of Canada.

He was appointed War Artist after enlisting with the RCAF in 1943 and spent the following two years recording his impressions of wartime England in 116 pencil drawings and watercolours.

Chosen for Canada's first participation in the Venice Biennale (1952) along with Emily Carr, David Milne and Alfred Pellan, he was also included in biennials in São Paulo (1951 and 1953), Mexico (1958) and Ottawa (1959). In 1954, under the patronage of the Canadian Embassy in Paris, he had a one-man exhibition at the Galérie R. Creuze. The National Gallery of Canada organized and circulated a retrospective in 1969-70 with a well-documented catalogue.

Goodridge Roberts held numerous teaching positions. In 1959 he was appointed first resident artist at the University of New Brunswick, in his home town of Fredericton, where he did his first series of winter landscapes along the St. John River, N.B., through the front window of his parked car.

He was awarded many distinctions: 1939 and 1957, the Jessie Dow Prize for watercolour; the Junior League Award, Winnipeg, 1957; the Glazebrook Award for landscape in the National Gallery's third Biennial of Canadian Art, 1959; an honorary Doctor of Laws degree at the University of New Brunswick, 1960.

He was a charter member of the Contemporary Art Society in Montreal and was elected to membership of both the Canadian Society of Painters in Water Colour and the Canadian Society of Graphic Art in 1939. In 1956 he became a member of the Royal Canadian Academy of Arts. That same year, his oil painting *Port au Persil* was chosen by the Royal Canadian Air Force Association for presentation to Her Majesty, Queen Elizabeth II.

Through all his career, Goodridge Roberts sought out the kind of Canadian landscapes that appealed to him to paint. With Alfred Pinsky, a fellow painter, he bought a farm near Calumet, Quebec in 1956. He also owned a cottage near Pointe-au-Baril, on Georgian Bay. At these two places, and at his home in Westmount, he continued to work until his death in March 1974 following a long illness.

Goodridge Roberts
How can I catch it
Running as it is before the terrible wind?
How can I intercept it
Fleeing the fury?
How can I block it, trip it,
How put an end to its dodging and doubling?

My hands cannot quite touch this body as it passes
With glance turned back bewildered and beseeching.
The forehead wet, the hair pushed straightly back
The mouth ajar and the scared heart panting.

It runs so swiftly, fox-like in its cunning
How can I stop it, how can I make it cease
This terrible motion, this running running away.
How can I call a halt, an end to madness?
How gather it into my arms
And turn it, turn its head
To that grove where the air lies dreaming
And primroses dot a field
Down to a bright river?

Goodridge Roberts; ©Joan Roberts

[2]*Canadian Art Magazine*, Summer, 1955

54. Goodridge Roberts
Laurentian Landscape, 1946
charcoal drawing on paper
18¹/₂ x 24¹/₂ in.   46.99 x 62.23 cm.

52. Goodridge Roberts
Laurentian Landscape, 1939
watercolour on paper
20½ x 24⅝ in.   52 x 62.9 cm.

Anne Douglas Savage   1896-1971

Anne Savage was born on July 27, 1896 in Montreal, where she was to live most of her life. She discovered the beauty of the countryside as a child when in 1908 her father bought a property in the Laurentians, and built a family home beside a lake. Lake Wonish, close to Sixteen Island Lake, is secluded and beautiful and here the family spent their summers. At this time not many people had summer houses so far north of Montreal. There were few roads and the only way to get there was by the train[1] which wound its way through the Laurentians.

From 1915 to 1918 Anne Savage studied at the Art Association of Montreal with William Brymner and Maurice Cullen, and from 1920 to 1921 at the Minneapolis School of Art. Her long teaching career began in 1921, and that same year she helped found the Beaver Hall Group of painters, a group

sharing studio space at Beaver Hall Square. Although this association lasted only about eighteen months, contacts and friendships from this time continued for many years.

The Baron Byng High School in Montreal opened in 1922, and Anne Savage took over the art department where she continued teaching until 1948. She spent some time in Toronto during 1923–1924, and worked with Arthur Lismer at the Ontario College of Art. In 1924 she visited Britain and France. In 1937 she began teaching children's art classes at the Montreal Art Association. She was appointed Assistant Supervisor of Art for the Protestant schools of Montreal in 1948, and Supervisor in 1951. She retired from active teaching in the summer of 1953. A founding member of the Canadian Group of Painters in 1933, she was president of the association in 1949 and again in 1960.

In the summer of 1927, Anne Savage, Pegi Nichol and the sculptor Florence Wyle were assigned by Marius Barbeau to make a visual record of the Indian totem poles that still existed on the Skeena River in British Columbia. Although Anne Savage travelled often – teaching in Banff, sketching and painting in eastern Quebec, joining A.Y. Jackson in a sketching party to Georgian Bay – her painting life was mainly centred on the Laurentians, particularly in and around her home at Lake Wonish.

She built herself a small studio where she would retreat during school holidays, sketching and painting the land around her – thick forest closing in around the lake, with grey boulders interrupting the uneven rhythm of the land. Vivid contrasts of colour – bright blue and greens of the summers, splashes of yellow made by her favourite sunflowers; earthy autumn browns and ochres – the mood changes of

the seasons and the rhythms of the landscape were what she essentially captured in her sketches and her paintings.

Anne Savage is remembered as an art educator but her painting was as vital to her as teaching. It offered her relief from a profession that demanded so much time and energy. Yet for her the two – teaching and painting – were intimately linked. Her pupils loved her and there is no doubt that she too thrived on the personal contact of teaching. Her desire to impart knowledge led her in 1939 to give a series of eight talks on Canadian art for the CBC.[2]

Over the years, Anne Savage's works have been exhibited in various group exhibitions, among them the British Empire Exhibition, Wembley, London, 1925; *Exposition d'Art Canadien* in 1927 at the Musée du Jeu de Paume, Paris; at the Corcoran Gallery, Washington, D.C., in an exhibition of paintings of contemporary Canadian artists in 1930; at the Coronation Exhibition, London, in 1935; at the Royal Institute Galleries, London, in an exhibition of paintings, drawings and sculptures by artists of the British Empire overseas, 1937; in 1938 *A Century of Canadian Art* at the Tate Gallery, London, and at Yale University Art Gallery, New Haven, Connecticut in 1944 in an exhibition *Canadian Art 1750-1943*. More recently, *Anne Savage A Retrospective* was organized by her former students at the Sir George Williams Art Galleries, Concordia University, Montreal in April 1969, and a second one-man exhibition *Annie D. Savage Drawings and Water-colours* was organized by that same institution and circulated through the Atlantic Provinces during 1974–75.

Anne D. Savage died in Montreal in 1971 after a period of illness.

[1]Fritz Brandtner's painting *Laurel in the Laurentians* shows the railway track on which the train would pass.

[2]Transcript in archives of Concordia University, Montreal.

Anne D. Savage

The part of the country which is my real locale is a little lake in the Laurentians. The country around the lake is very undulating with little ravines and hills so that without going far you could sit down, turn your back and you would have a completely new composition. The whole thing was compacted. I think perhaps it was harder to know, to get the variety of what to paint. Down at the sea you had rocks, villages and back country. In the Laurentians you only had trees and reflections and lakes, and I had friends who would come up to paint there and they couldn't do it at all.... All you can do is separate the lights from the darks of that foliage. I found it a challenge because I found a great deal of variety in it.... This particular lake [Wonish] has something quite extraordinary about it. It has beautiful closeups, very intimate.... It made me dig a lot harder than if I had just gone to an obvious place to paint.

Transcript of tape for *Anne Savage, Teacher* by Arthur H. Calvin. Thesis, Sir George Williams University, 1969

56. Anne Savage
Lake Wonish, Thanksgiving, c. 1945
oil on wood
12 x 14 in.   30.48 x 35.56 cm.

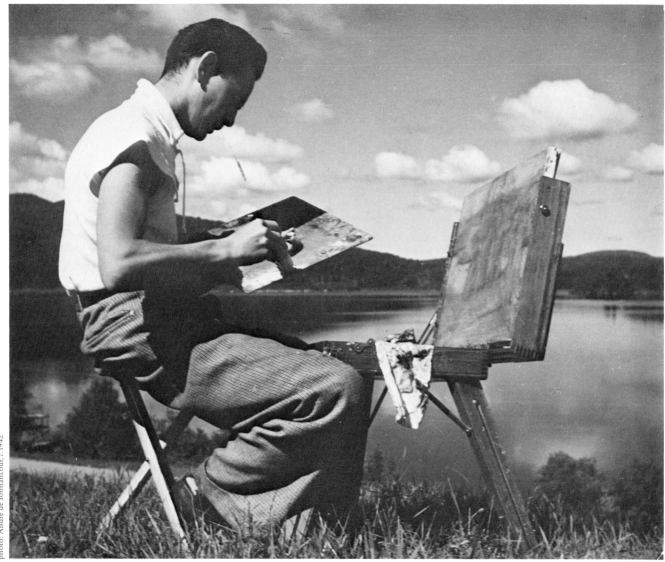

photo: André de Tonnancour, c.1942

72

Jacques de Tonnancour   1917-

Jacques de Tonnancour was born in January 1917 in Montreal, son of a doctor. He experienced the pleasure of the countryside early in his life, spending every summer from the age of five at his parents' cottage at St Donat. As a boy he was fascinated by insects. By observing them and looking for them, he became more and more aware of the wider world around them. Absorbed by the 'close-up,' the detail, the intimacy, he did not 'see' the landscape as such. This deep interest in entomology led to de Tonnancour's enrolment at the Ecole des Beaux-arts in 1937, with the intention of becoming an illustrator of scientific books.

In pursuing his studies he began to feel a growing difficulty in remaining factual, in disciplining himself to override the aesthetic reason for drawing, to suppress the impulse to include feeling in order to maintain meticulous attention to organic facts. Drawn toward freer art forms, he began to study art for art's sake. Then he came to feel that the approach to teaching at the Ecole des Beaux-arts was unsatisfactory. In 1939, encouraged by his father, he began painting on his own, compelled as he was to express himself in larger format, and to draw on his own inventiveness and imagination.

Concurrent with his painting, in about 1941, he began writing critical reviews and articles in magazines and newspapers, a practice which he continued to do for the next quarter of a century. Les Editions de l'Arbre brought out a biography, *G. Roberts*, in 1944, written by de Tonnancour.

Among his friends were Alfred Pellan, Paul-Emile Borduas, and Goodridge Roberts. Roberts shared de Tonnancour's feeling and response towards the Laurentians and strongly affected his early style of landscape painting.

De Tonnancour's first one-man exhibition was held in 1942 at the Dominion Gallery, Montreal, and *Jeune Fille Assise* was bought by The National Gallery of Canada. That same year he began teaching at the Montreal School of Art and Design, then directed by Arthur Lismer. At this time, too, he became a member of the Contemporary Art Society. This period was productive, and his works were exhibited in Montreal and Toronto.

He was awarded a scholarship by the Brazilian government in 1945 which gave him a year in Brazil, mainly Rio de Janeiro. The insects and butterflies that had been such a preoccupation of his childhood when he dreamt of foreign lands and forests where exotic species lived were now forgotten. Painting was all-important.

After his return to Canada in 1946, and until 1950, he concentrated mainly on still life and figure painting. Many works of this period were acquired by museums across the country. De Tonnancour shared an exhibition at The Montreal Museum of Fine Arts in 1949 with Albert Dumouchel; their friendship and association proved to be an important influence on de Tonnancour and his work.

In 1950, he attended the Fifth UNESCO Conference in Florence. At this time he was worried that his work was becoming formalistic and derivative of the style of painting associated with Picasso. He almost stopped painting between 1950 to 1955, because he needed time in which to re-assess the basic criteria of his art. He moved to St Lambert where he built a home and studio. Then he returned to the Ecole des Beaux-arts in Montreal as a teacher.

Four years later, de Tonnancour began painting again. Later, referring to the time when he experienced this personal crisis towards his painting, he said: *At a certain moment in 1955 after four years when I couldn't paint at all, I went back to the Laurentians for a week and just bathed in the landscape. It gave me an urge to come back to an earlier stage when I was influenced by Goodridge Roberts.*[1]

This marked the beginning of his most productive period and a return to landscape painting, landscapes which were never executed *sur place*, but were assimilated and then interpreted in his way.

He exhibited widely – at The Montreal Museum of Fine Arts in 1956 with Louis Archambault; at Laing Gallery, Toronto, in 1956, 1958 and 1962; in Australia in 1957; at the Canadian Exhibition, World's Fair, Brussels, and the Venice Biennale in 1958; in Germany, Switzerland and Mexico. Back home in Montreal, exhibitions of his work were held at the Galerie Denyse Delrue in 1958, 1959 and 1960.

De Tonnancour's landscape paintings became progressively more simplified until in 1960 his "squeegee" technique enabled him to abstract further the landscape. This led him on to actual abstract painting, to creating different materials for collage. His works continued to be widely exhibited: a major retrospective was held at the Vancouver Art Gallery in 1966. That same year he undertook the mural at the Dow Planetarium, Montreal, and in 1968 he embarked on a series of sculptures and integrated murals for the University of Montreal. He had one-man exhibitions at the Galerie Agnes Lefort, Montreal, and the Dunkelman Gallery, Toronto, in

[1]Interview with M. Ebbitt Cutler, *Canadian Art*, Jan./Feb. 1965

1969; that year, too, he was appointed artist-in-residence at the University of Quebec in Montreal. His most recent one-man exhibition was held at the Galerie Marlborough Godard, Montreal, in 1975.

Jacques de Tonnancour
I rediscovered, on the way back going through the spruce forests, in the muskeg country and elsewhere, this linear graphic quality in the forests and my painting developed as a graphic embroidery running through space. This was only incidental because this only brought back a kind of obsession I've had with forests, with vegetation, with the outdoors which I have known in the Laurentians since I was a child. So I think that on the whole it is a question for the artist of reaching deeply into this level where the first images have marked you and I think that those are the most profound contents you want to be tied with until the end of your life. It's a question of expanding and maturing over them. But this return to childhood images is essential to any artist if he wants to make his way at the period of maturity.

Canadian Conference of the Arts, 1961
Discussion of the visual arts
Canadian Art, September/October 1961

My Laurentian landscape series was about silence and a feeling of timelessness expressed through a slow progression into the depth of the scene.

In the Sixties I abandoned figuration and depth of space for a strict flatness. Was I then forsaking the very essence of my thematic aims?

This worried me a little until I came to understand that if I was no longer painting depth in space I was finally painting what I always tried to paint: depth in time, duration, timelessness, but now in a direct way.

J. de Tonnancour
October 1976

61. Jacques de Tonnancour
At the Foot of the Mountain, 1963
oil on presswood
15⅞ x 23¾ in.   40.13 x 60.33 cm.

60. Jacques de Tonnancour
Laurentian Heave, 1959
oil on masonite
35½ x 47 in.   90.17 x 119.38 cm.

Catalogue of the Exhibition

1. André Biéler
Early Spring in the Laurentians, 1929
oil on canvas
20 x 26¼ in. 50.8 x 66.7 cm.
Lent by Mr. and Mrs. Jean Biéler

2. André Biéler
St Sauveur, 1930
conté and watercolour wash on paper
5³⁄₈ x 7 in. 13.4 x 17.6 cm.
Lent by the artist

3. André Biéler
Morning Sun, St Sauveur, 1930
pencil and watercolour wash on paper
4⁵⁄₈ x 5¼ in. 11.6 x 13.3 cm.
Lent by the artist

4. André Biéler
St Sauveur, c. 1931
conté on paper
5¼ x 7 in. 13.4 x 17.7 cm.
Lent by the artist

5. André Biéler
Horses and Sleigh, c. 1931
conté on paper
5¼ x 7 in. 13.4 x 17.8 cm.
Lent by the artist

6. André Biéler
The Pub, St Sauveur, 1932
pencil on paper
5¼ x 7 in. 13.4 x 17.8 cm.
Lent by the artist

7. André Biéler
St Sauveur, 1932
pencil and watercolour on paper
5¼ x 7 in. 13.4 x 17.5 cm.
Lent by the artist

8. André Biéler
St Sauveur, 1932
coloured crayon and conté on paper
5⁷⁄₈ x 9 in. 14.8 x 22.6 cm.
Lent by the artist

9. André Biéler
St Sauveur, 1932
coloured crayon and conté on paper
7 x 10½ in. 17.8 x 26.5 cm.
Lent by the artist

10. André Biéler
St Sauveur, 1932
coloured crayon on paper
7 x 10½ in. 17.8 x 26.5 cm.
Lent by the artist

11. André Biéler
St Sauveur des Monts, 1932
coloured crayon and conté on paper
7 x 10½ in. 17.8 x 26.3 cm.
Lent by the artist

12. André Biéler
Voting at Ste Adèle, 1937
ink and watercolour on card
5½ x 6¼ in. 13.8 x 15.8 cm.
Lent by the artist

13. André Biéler
Rivière du Nord, 1937
oil on canvas
42½ x 46 in. 107.9 x 116.8 cm.
Lent by the artist

14. André Biéler
Election Day, Ste Adèle, 1938
watercolour on paper
19³⁄₈ x 24¹⁄₈ in. 49.21 x 61.28 cm.
Collection Art Gallery of Ontario
Purchase, 1938

15. Sam Borenstein
Ste Marguerite Station, P.Q., 1943
oil on canvas
28 x 46 in. 71.12 x 116.84 cm.
Lent by Mrs. Judith Borenstein

16. Sam Borenstein
Village Québecois, 1966
tempera on paper
30 x 40 in. 76.2 x 101.6 cm.
Lent by Mrs. Judith Borenstein

17. Fritz Brandtner
Laurel in the Laurentians, 1934
pastel and ink on paper
10 x 12½ in. 25.4 x 31.75 cm.
Lent by Paul Kastel, Kastel Gallery Inc.

18. Fritz Brandtner
Sixteen Islands, Laurentian Mountains, c. 1934/35
pastel and ink on paper
11½ x 14¼ in. 29.21 x 26.2 cm.
Lent by Paul Kastel, Kastel Gallery Inc.

19. Fritz Brandtner
Sixteen Islands Lake (No 1), 1942
watercolour on paper
18¹⁄₁₆ x 24 in. 45.9 x 61 cm.
Collection Art Gallery of Ontario
Purchase, 1943

20. Fritz Brandtner
Fall, n.d.
watercolour on paper
19½ x 24¹⁄₈ in. 49.5 x 61.3 cm.
Lent by the Art Gallery of Hamilton

21. Maurice Cullen
La Rivière du nord, 1932
oil on canvas
30¼ x 40 in. 76.8 x 101.6 cm.
Lent by The Montreal Museum of Fine Arts
Purchased 1932
Dr. & Mrs. Charles F. Martin Fund

22. **Maurice Cullen**
Evening on the Caché River, n.d.
pastel on paper
25 x 33 in.   63.5 x 83.82 cm.
Lent by the Saint James's Club of Montreal

23. **Maurice Cullen**
Laurentian Hills, n.d.
oil on canvas
22½ x 27½ in.   57.15 x 69.85 cm.
Lent by Nipissing University College

24. **Marc-Aurèle Fortin**
Pastorale, 1928
watercolour
23 x 27⁶/10 in.   58 x 70 cm.
Lent by Jean Allaire, Q.C.

25. **Marc-Aurèle Fortin**
Vue de Lesage, Laurentides, c.1938
oil on canvas
51⅛ x 67 in.   130 x 170 cm.
Lent by the Power Corporation of Canada

26. **Marc-Aurèle Fortin**
Paysage, n.d.
oil on canvas
24 x 38¼ in.   61 x 97.1 cm.
Lent by the Musée du Québec

27. **Edwin Holgate**
Morin Heights, 1927
oil on board
11 x 16 in.   27.94 x 40.64 cm.
Lent by Paul Kastel, Kastel Gallery Inc.

28. **Edwin Holgate**
Lac Tremblant, c. 1930
oil on canvas
26 x 34 in.   66.04 x 86.36 cm.
Lent by Gerald W. Schwartz

29. **Edwin Holgate**
Laurentian Cemetery, c. 1948
pencil drawing
12½ x 16½ in.   31.75 x 41.91 cm.
Lent by the artist, courtesy of the Walter Klinkhoff Gallery, Inc.

30. **Edwin Holgate**
Laurentian Cemetery, July 16, 1948
ink and crayon on paper
12½ x 16½ in.   31.75 x 41.91 cm.
Lent by the artist, courtesy of the Walter Klinkhoff Gallery, Inc.

31. **Edwin Holgate**
Laurentian Cemetery, 1948
oil on panel
8½ x 10½ in.   21.6 x 26.7 cm.
Collection Art Gallery of Ontario
Purchase, 1957

32. **Edwin Holgate**
Laurentian Cemetery, 1949
oil on board
20⅛ x 24 in.   51.1 x 61 cm.
Lent by The Montreal Museum of Fine Arts
Purchased 1964
Horsley & Annie Townsend Bequest

33. **Edwin Holgate**
Mountain Scene, 1929
oil on canvas
24 x 29 in.   60.96 x 73.66 cm.
Lent by the University Club of Montreal

34. **Patrick Landsley**
Winter Light, 1973
oil and acrylic on canvas
69 x 54 in.   175.26 x 137.16 cm.
Lent by the artist

35. **Patrick Landsley**
Winter Eclipse, 1975
coloured pencil, charcoal and pencil on paper
11½ x 12½ in.   29.21 x 31.75 cm.
Lent by the artist

36. **John Lyman**
Oat Field in the Laurentians, 1942
oil on wood
14¹⁵/16 x 18⅛ in.   38 x 46 cm.
Lent by the Musée du Québec

37. **John Lyman**
St Jovite, n.d.
watercolour on paper
9⅜ x 11⅞ in.   46.99 x 30.16 cm. (sight)
Lent by Dr. and Mrs. Max Stern, Dominion Gallery, Montreal

38. **John Lyman**
Haying by the Lake, n.d.
oil on canvas
18 x 22 in.   45.7 x 55.8 cm.
Lent by The Montreal Museum of Fine Arts
Gift of Thornton Grier, 1939

39. **Louis Muhlstock**
Laurentian Interior, Val Morin, 1938
oil on canvas
26 x 30 in.   66.04 x 76.2 cm.
Lent by the artist

40. **Louis Muhlstock**
Laurentian Boulders, 1973
brown (sepia) chalk (slight wash) on paper
20 x 26 in.   50.8 x 66.04 cm.
Lent by the artist

41. **Louis Muhlstock**
Autumn (Isola) Val David, Laurentians, 1975
oil on canvas board
16 x 20 in.   40.64 x 50.8 cm.
Lent by the artist

42. **Louis Muhlstock**
Laurentians, First Snow (Fragment), 1975
oil on canvas board
18 x 14 in.   45.72 x 35.56 cm.
Lent by the artist

43. **Roland Pichet**
Three images and one poem from
Suite Québecoise: blues pour un piquet de clôture, 1975
serigraphs
13 x 20 in.   33.02 x 50.8 cm. each
Lent by the artist

44. **Roland Pichet**
Ce Pays, 1976
oil on canvas
6 x 72 in.   15.24 x 182.88 cm.
Lent by the artist

45. **Robert Pilot**
Laurentian Scene, late 30s
oil on board, painted on both sides
9 x 12 in.   22.86 x 30.48 cm.
Lent by John Langdon

46. **Robert Pilot**
Lac Supérieur, P.Q., c. 1946
oil on canvas
21½ x 27½ in.   54.61 x 69.85 cm.
Lent by The Hamilton Club

47. **Jean-Paul Riopelle**
Untitled, 1974
oil on canvas
57½ x 38¼ in.   146.05 x 97.16 cm.
Lent by Joseph Kerzner

48. **Jean-Paul Riopelle**
Untitled, 1976
ink on paper
26 x 21½ in.   66 x 54.6 cm.
Lent by the artist, courtesy of the Gilles Corbeil
Gallery

49. **Jean-Paul Riopelle**
Untitled, 1976
ink on paper
21½ x 26 in.   54.6 x 66 cm.
Lent by the artist, courtesy of the Gilles Corbeil
Gallery

50. **Jean-Paul Riopelle**
Untitled, 1976
ink on paper
21½ x 26 in.   54.6 x 66 cm.
Lent by the artist, courtesy of the Gilles Corbeil
Gallery

51. **Jean-Paul Riopelle**
Untitled, 1976
ink on paper
21½ x 26 in.   54.6 x 66 cm.
Lent by the artist, courtesy of the Gilles Corbeil
Gallery

52. **Goodridge Roberts**
Laurentian Landscape, 1939
watercolour on paper
20½ x 24⅝ in.   52 x 62.9 cm.
Lent by The Montreal Museum of Fine Arts
Purchased 1940, Cheney Fund

53. **Goodridge Roberts**
Hillside, St Alphonse, 1942
oil on canvas
19½ x 29½ in.   49.53 x 74.93 cm.
Lent by Mrs. Joan Roberts

54. **Goodridge Roberts**
Laurentian Landscape, 1946
charcoal drawing on paper
18½ x 24½ in.   46.99 x 62.23 cm.
Lent by Mrs. Joan Roberts

55. **Goodridge Roberts**
Landscape, Morin Heights, 1953
oil on masonite
32 x 45 in.   81.28 x 114.3 cm.
Lent by Mrs. Joan Roberts

56. **Anne Savage**
Lake Wonish, Thanksgiving, c.1945
oil on wood
12 x 14 in.   30.48 x 35.56 cm.
Lent by Mr. and Mrs. R.L. McDougall

57. **Anne Savage**
Lake Wonish, Easter, c.1945
oil on wood
12 x 14 in.   30.48 x 35.56 cm.
Lent by Mr. and Mrs. R.L. McDougall

58. **Anne Savage**
July, Wonish, 1960
oil on masonite
33 x 48 in.   83.82 x 121.92 cm.
Lent by John B. Claxton

59. **Jacques de Tonnancour**
Paysage de juin, 1957
oil on panel
31¼ x 43¾ in.   79.4 x 111.1 cm.
Lent by The National Gallery of Canada, Ottawa

60. **Jacques de Tonnancour**
Laurentian Heave, 1959
oil on masonite
35½ x 47 in.   90.17 x 119.38 cm.
Lent by Maclean-Hunter Limited

61. **Jacques de Tonnancour**
At the Foot of the Mountain, 1963
oil on presswood
15⅞ x 23¾ in.   40.13 x 60.33 cm.
Lent by Hart House Permanent Collection

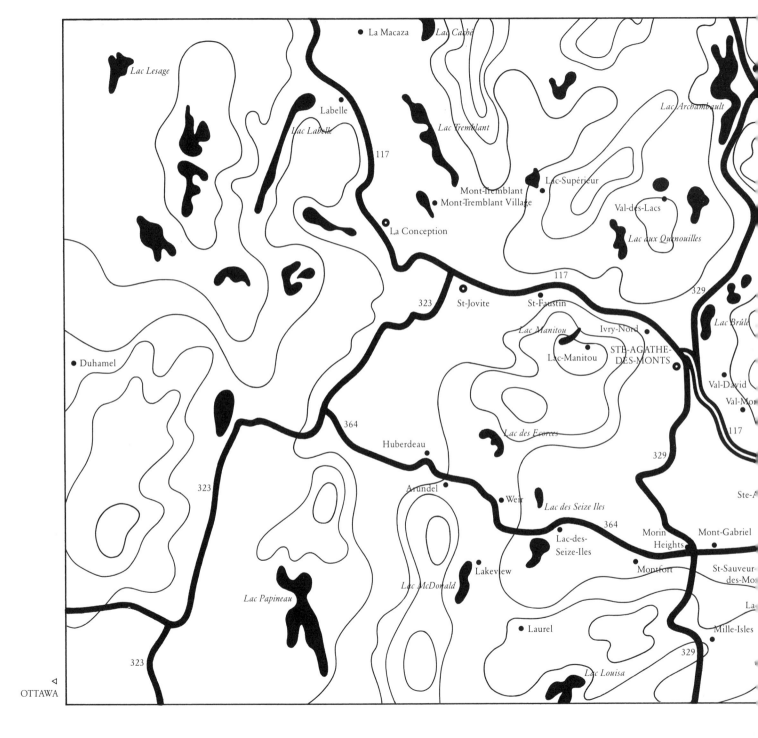

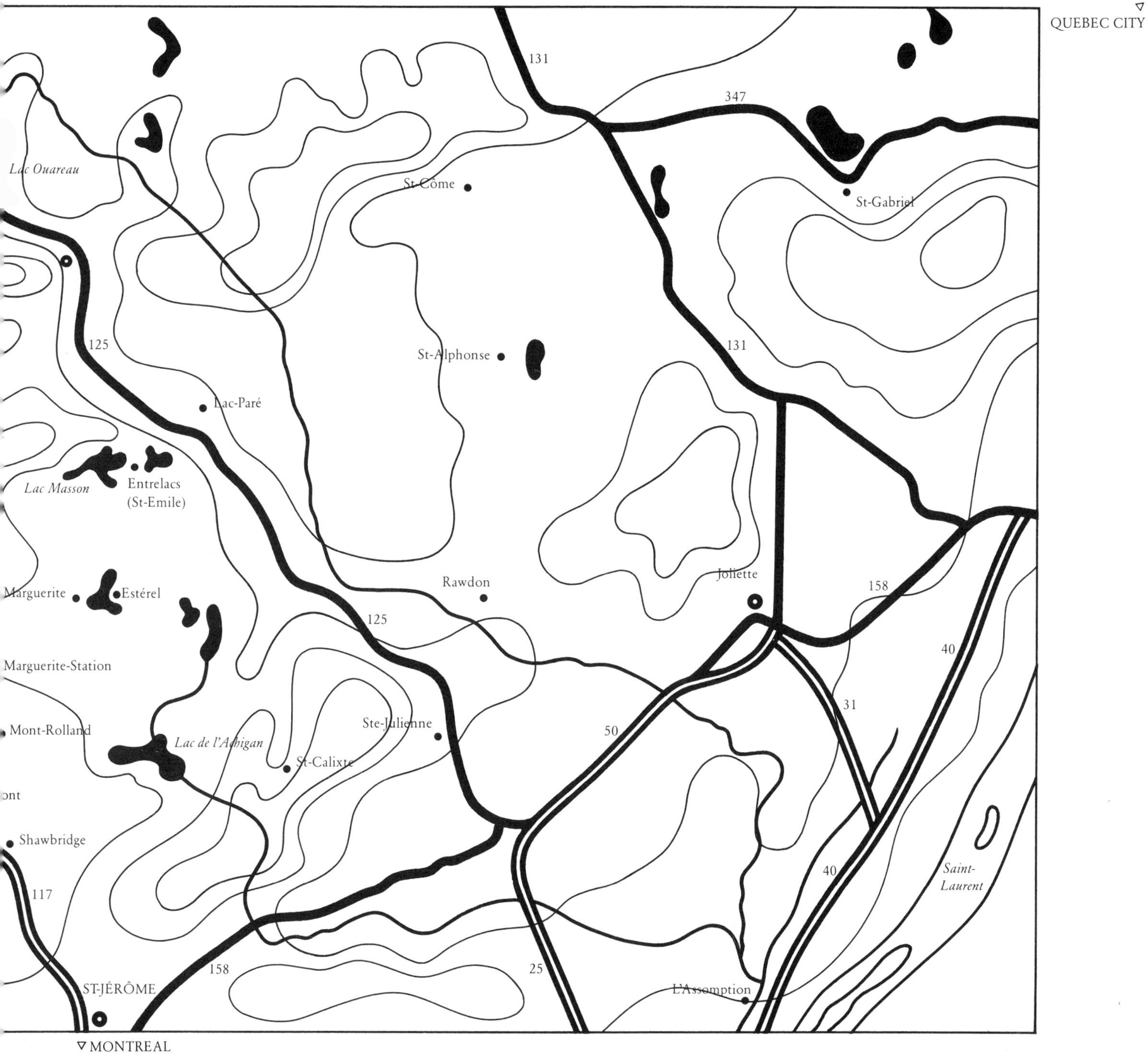

QUEBEC CITY

131

347

St-Côme

St-Gabriel

Lac Ouareau

125

St-Alphonse

Lac-Paré

131

Lac Masson

Entrelacs
(St-Emile)

Joliette

Rawdon

158

Marguerite

Estérel

40

Marguerite-Station

31

Mont-Rolland

Lac de l'Achigan

Ste-Julienne

50

St-Calixte

ont

40

Saint-
Laurent

Shawbridge

117

158

25

L'Assomption

ST-JÉRÔME

▽ MONTREAL

81

1. André Biéler
Early Spring in the Laurentians, 1929

33. Edwin Holgate
Mountain Scene, 1929

Biéler/Holgate

Dialogue between André Biéler and Edwin Holgate about painting together on Constantino Hill in March 1929.

AB End of March, we stayed at a friend's house in Manitou where the Laurentians are very hilly, accented with trees and just made for sketching.

EH Actually a heat spell. I remember a swarm of wild bees suddenly buzzing around us.

AB Almost impossible to move around, although I remember we climbed one day, successfully, one of the high hills and there in the forest was this marvellous slope, might have been on the north slope, where there was a great accumulation of snow and we both did sketches, and yours was really a lovely thing, which you developed into an important canvas.

EH Constantino's hill, the spring break-up.

AB Our paintings are quite similar but quite different in character. Yours was very cool, the cool snow, the cool sky, and on the contrary mine was a sunset kind of thing. It's very warm, and the snow is very warm. I remember the contrast.

Interview with André Biéler, Edwin Holgate and Frances K. Smith, September 29, 1968.

Bibliography

General Works

Buchanan, Donald W.   *The Growth of Canadian Painting,* Collins, London/Toronto, 1950

Duval, Paul   *Four Decades,* Clarke Irwin & Co. Ltd., Toronto, 1972

Harper, J. Russell   *Paintings in Canada   A History,* University of Toronto Press, 1966

Hill, Charles C.   *Canadian Painting in the Thirties,* exhibition catalogue, The National Gallery of Canada, Ottawa, 1975

Hubbard, R.H.   *Canadian Painting: The Forerunners,* Canadian Art Today, Studio International , 1970

Hubbard, R.H., and Ostiguy, Jean-René   *Three Hundred Years of Canadian Art,* exhibition catalogue, Queen's Printer, Ottawa, 1967

MacDonald, Colin S.   *A Dictionary of Canadian Artists,* Vols. 1–4, Canadian Paperbacks, Ottawa

Reid, Dennis   *A Concise History of Canadian Painting,* Toronto, Oxford University Press, 1973

Robert, Guy   *L'Art au Québec depuis 1940,* Les Editions La Presse, Ottawa, 1973

Saint-Martin, Fernande   *Trois générations d'art québecois,* exhibition catalogue, Musée d'Art contemporain, Montreal, 1976

Watson, William R.   *Retrospective Recollections of a Montreal Art Dealer,* University of Toronto Press, 1974

Encyclopaedia of the Arts, Editor: Herbert Read, Meredith Press, New York, 1966

Works on Individual Artists

André Biéler

Allen, Ralph   *André Biéler   50 years: a retrospective exhibition 1920-1970,* exhibition catalogue, Agnes Etherington Art Centre, Kingston, 1970

Ayre, Robert   *André Biéler   A Retrospective Exhibition of Work from 1925 to 1963,* exhibition catalogue, Agnes Etherington Art Centre, Kingston, 1963

Biéler, André   "Mural of the Saguenay," *Canadian Art,* Vol. IX, No. 2, 1951

Conversations with Mr. and Mrs. André Biéler, January and September 1976

Sam Borenstein

Ayre, Robert   *The Standard,* Montreal, November 11, 1939

Ayre, Robert   *Montreal Star,* May 20, 1950; December 18, 1954; March 12, 1965; November 2, 1966

Brace, Brock   *The Varsity,* Toronto, October 5, 1943

Forster, Michael   *The Standard,* Montreal, September 16, 1950

Horner, Stan   *The Gazette,* Montreal, November 5, 1966

Kirshner, Sheldon   *The Westward News,* September 3, 1964

McCarthy, Pearl   *The Gazette,* Montreal, November 6, 1943

Newman, Ernest   *Canadian Jewish Year Book,* 1940

Pfeiffer, Dorothy   *The Gazette,* Montreal, October 26, 1963

The Canadian Forum, August 1935

Saturday Night, Toronto, March 1937; April 1939

The Evening Telegram, Toronto, March 22, 1939

The Gazette, Montreal, April 19, 1941

World Affairs, Toronto, December 1941

Montreal Star, November 8, 1967

Sam Borenstein, exhibition catalogue, Art Gallery of Hamilton, September, 1974

Fritz Brandtner

Abell, Walter   "War Industry Drawings by Muhlstock and Brandtner," *Canadian Art,* October/November 1943

Ayre, Robert
Denechaud, Jean
Duval, Paul   *Montreal Star,* April 15, 1950

La Presse, Montreal, April 27, 1950

Saturday Night, December 1, 1948

Harper, J. Russell   *Fritz Brandtner 1896-1969, A Retrospective Exhibition,* exhibition catalogue, Sir George Williams University, Montreal, 1971

White, Michael   *The Gazette,* Montreal, March 13, 1971

Personal notebooks of Fritz Brandtner
Conversation with Mrs. Mieze Brandtner, July 1976.

Maurice Cullen

Burgoyne, St. George   *The Gazette,* Montreal, March 29, 1934

Laberge, Jean Albert   *Peintres et Ecrivains d'hier et d'aujourd'hui,* edition privée, Montreal, 1928

Pilot, Robert   Transcript of lecture at the National Gallery of Canada, Ottawa, July 1948

Pilot, Robert   *Maurice Cullen 1866-1934,* exhibition catalogue, Art Gallery of Hamilton, 1956

Sutton, Denys   *James William Morrice,* exhibition catalogue, a loan exhibition arranged for the Bath Festival, England, by The National Gallery of Canada, Ottawa, 1968

Marc-Aurèle Fortin

Barbeau, Marius   *Painters of Quebec,* The Ryerson Press, 1946

Bonneville, Jean-Pierre   *M.A. Fortin,* exhibition catalogue, Verdun Cultural Centre, May 1968

Chauvin, Jean   *Ateliers,* Louis Carrier & Cie., Les Editions du Mercure, Montreal, 1928

Ostiguy, Jean-René   "Marc-Aurèle Fortin," *Vie des Arts,* No. 23, Montreal, 1961

Ostiguy, Jean-René   *Fortin,* exhibition catalogue, The National Gallery of Canada, Ottawa, 1964

Robert, Guy   *Marc-Aurèle Fortin, l'homme à l'œuvre,* Les Editions Internationales Alain Stanké, Ottawa, 1976

Edwin Holgate

Heywood, Irene   *The Gazette,* Montreal, September 26, 1970

Kritzwiser, Kay   *The Globe and Mail,* Toronto, August 19, 1975

Shapiro, Betty   *The Gazette,* Montreal, August 10, 1973

Reid, Dennis   *Edwin Holgate: Paintings,* text accompanying exhibition, The National Gallery of Canada, Ottawa, 1975

Reid, Dennis   *Edwin H. Holgate,* Canadian Artists Series, The National Gallery of Canada, Ottawa, 1976

The Gazette, Montreal, November 4, 1937
Conversations with Mr. and Mrs. E. Holgate
November 1975, May 1976, October 1976

Patrick Landsley

Roussan, Jacques de   Perspectives-dimanches, *Dimanche Matin,* February 1975

Conversations with Patrick Landsley, November 1975, May 1976, November 1976

John Lyman

Ayre, Robert   *The Montrealer,* February, 1937

Corbeil, Gilles   "John Lyman," *Arts et Pensée,* Jan/Feb. 1954

Dumas, Paul   *Lyman,* Les Editions de l'Arbre, Montreal, 1944

Humphrey, John P.   "Lyman," *Le Quartier Latin,* December 17, 1943

Morgan-Powell, S.   *Montreal Star,* May 23, 1943

Robillard, Ives   *La Presse,* Montreal, January 21, 1967

Surrey, Philip   *Hommage à John Lyman à l'occasion de ses 80 ans,* exhibition catalogue, Musée du Québec, November, 1966

The Gazette, Montreal, May 29, 1967
John Lyman Journals, Bibliothèque Nationale du Québec

Louis Muhlstock

Ayre, Robert	"Louis Muhlstock," *Northern Review,* Vol. 2 No. 4, 1949
Ayre, Robert	"The New Muhlstock," *Canadian Art,* Vol. IX, No. 4, Summer 1952
Dumas, Paul, and Hill, Charles C.	*Louis Muhlstock A Survey of Forty-Five Years,* exhibition catalogue, Art Gallery of Windsor, 1976
Macartney, C.A.	*The Habsburg Empire 1790-1918,* Weidenfeld & Nicolson, London, 1968
Repentigny, Rodolphe de	"Louis Muhlstock," *Vie des Arts,* No. 16, Autumn 1959
Sabbath, Lawrence	Interview with Louis Muhlstock, *Canadian Art,* Vol. XVII, No. 4, July 1960
Saumier, Monique	*Louis Muhlstock: Un demi-siècle de Peinture,* Thesis, Concordia University, Montreal, March 1975
	Conversations with Louis Muhlstock, October 1976

Robert Pilot

Duval, Paul	*Hamilton Spectator,* January 25, 1969
MacDonald, T.R.	*Robert W. Pilot Retrospective,* exhibition catalogue, The Montreal Museum of Fine Arts, 1968
Sabbath, Lawrence	Interview with Robert Pilot, *Canadian Art,* Vol. XVIII, No. 5, Sept/Oct. 1961
Thériault, Normand	*La Presse,* Montreal, November 9, 1968
	The Gazette, Montreal, November 6, 1934; February 1, 1947 *Montreal Star,* February 4, 1947

Roland Pichet

McCutcheon, Sarah E.	"Roland Pichet," *Artscanada,* Oct/Nov. 1971
Shapiro, Betty	*The Gazette,* Montreal, August 9, 1973
	Conversations with Roland Pichet, November 1975, May, August and October 1976

Jean-Paul Riopelle

Auster, Paul	*Riopelle,* exhibition catalogue, Pierre Matisse Gallery, New York, November 1975
Duthuit, Georges	"A Painter of Awakening–Jean-Paul Riopelle," *Canadian Art,* Vol. X, No. 1, 1952
Lamy, Laurent	"Un peintre québecois connu dans le monde entier, Riopelle," interview, Hydro-Québec, *Forces,* No. 28, 1974
Michel, Jacques	"Le Retour de Riopelle," *Le Monde,* Paris, September 13, 1972
Robert, Guy	*Riopelle,* Les Editions de l'Homme, Montreal 1970
Russoli, Franco	Venice Biennial Catalogue, 1962
Schneider, Pierre	*Riopelle,* exhibition catalogue, includes *Au Louvre avec Riopelle,* interview with Pierre Schneider, Musée du Québec, 1967
	Riopelle, Maeght Editeur, Paris 1972 Conversations with Jean-Paul Riopelle, December 1975, July 1976, October 1976

Goodridge Roberts

Borcoman, James	*Goodridge Roberts A Retrospective Exhibition* with essays by Robert Ayre and Alfred Pinsky, The National Gallery of Canada, Ottawa, 1969-1970
Roberts, Goodridge	"From this point I looked out," *Queen's Quarterly,* Autumn 1953
Roberts, Goodridge	"A Report from Canada Fellowship Holders," *Canadian Art,* Summer 1955
Tonnancour, Jacques de	*G. Roberts,* Les Editions de l'Arbre, Montreal, 1944
	Conversations with Mrs. Joan Roberts, November 1975, February, May, October 1976

Anne Savage

Andrus, Donald F.P.	*Annie D. Savage Drawing and Watercolours,* Sir George Williams Art Galleries, Concordia University, Montreal 1974-75
Ayre, Robert	*Montreal Star,* April 12, 1967
Calvin, Arthur H.	*Anne Savage, Teacher,* Thesis, Sir George Williams University, 1967
Savage, Anne	Transcript of series of talks on Canadian Art for the CBC, 1939
Sherman, Leah	*Anne Savage, A Retrospective,* Sir George Williams Art Galleries, Concordia University, Montreal, April 1969
	La Presse, April 12, 1969 Conversations with Mrs. Robert McDougall, August and October 1976

Jacques de Tonnancour

Ayre, Robert	*Montreal Star,* January 21, 1956; March 1, 1958
Cutler, M. Ebbitt	Interview with Jacques de Tonnancour, *Canadian Art,* Vol. XXII, No. 1, Jan/Feb. 1965
Doyon, Charles	*Le Jour,* Montreal, April 17, 1943
Folch-Ribas, Jacques	*Jacques de Tonnancour, Le Signe et le Temps,* Collection Studio Les Presses de l'Université du Québec, 1971
Fulford, Robert	"De Tonnancour's Curious Crisis," *Mayfair,* January 1957
Shadbolt, Doris, and Simmins, Richard	*Jacques de Tonnancour,* exhibition catalogue, Vancouver Art Gallery, 1966
Tonnancour, Jacques de	"Should it be How to Paint or What to Paint?" *Canadian Art,* Vol. XIII, No. 3, Spring 1956
Tonnancour, Jacques de	"On Humanity in Canadian Art," *Canadian Art,* Vol. VII, No. 1, Autumn, 1959
	Canadian Conference of the Arts, 1961 *Canadian Art,* Vol. XVIII, No. 5, Sept/Oct. 1961 Conversations with Jacques de Tonnancour February and October 1976

Glossary

The Art Association of Montreal until 1948; *The Montreal Museum of Fine Arts* thereafter.

The *Art Gallery of Toronto* until 1966; the *Art Gallery of Ontario* thereafter.

Canadian Art magazine until 1966; *Artscanada* thereafter.

Sir George Williams University until August 1974; *Concordia University* thereafter.

Monument National: located on St Lawrence Boulevard, this institution served as a focal point for cultural and educational activities, specifically for French Canadians and francophiles. Classes in a variety of subjects were available free of charge.

Sketch box and palette used by **J.W. Morrice,** handed
on by him to **Maurice Cullen,** then to **Robert Pilot,**
then to **André Biéler.** Box 6¼″ x 7½″
Photo: Frances K. Smith

Lenders to the Exhibition

Jean Allaire, Q.C.

Art Gallery of Hamilton

Art Gallery of Ontario, Toronto

André Biéler

Mr. and Mrs. Jean Biéler

Mrs. Judith Borenstein

John B. Claxton

The Hamilton Club

Hart House Permanent Collection, University of Toronto

Edwin Holgate, courtesy of Walter Klinkhoff Gallery, Inc., Montreal

Paul Kastel, Kastel Gallery Inc., Montreal

Joseph Kerzner

Patrick Landsley

John Langdon

Maclean-Hunter Limited, Toronto

Mr. and Mrs. R. L. McDougall

The Montreal Museum of Fine Arts

Louis Muhlstock

Musée du Québec

The National Gallery of Canada, Ottawa

Nipissing University College, North Bay

Roland Pichet

Power Corporation of Canada, Montreal

Jean-Paul Riopelle, courtesy of the Gilles Corbeil Gallery, Montreal

Mrs. Joan Roberts

Saint James's Club of Montreal

Gerald W. Schwartz

Dr. and Mrs. Max Stern, Dominion Gallery, Montreal

University Club of Montreal

Biographical texts: Mela Constantinidi and
Helen Duffy
Design: Scott Thornley, Art Gallery of Ontario
Graphic Production: Meiko Bae, Art Gallery of Ontario
Design Assistance: Carol Sternberg, Art Gallery of Ontario
Map: Hiro Sugino
Typesetting: Goodtypes Incorporated
Printed by: Yorkville Press Limited
Colour separations: Empress Litho Limited

Photographs of the artists taken for the catalogue:
Gabor Szilasi: Louis Muhlstock
Basil Zarov: Patrick Landsley, Roland Pichet,
Jean-Paul Riopelle
Photography of art works:
Art Gallery of Ontario, No. 31
Neuville Bazin, Musée du Québec, No. 26
Lloyd Bloom Photography, Hamilton, No. 46
James A. Chambers, Art Gallery of Ontario, Nos. 14, 20, 24
Charlie King, Lachine, Québec, Nos. 17, 18
Piroska Mihalka, No. 35
The Montreal Museum of Fine Arts, Nos. 21, 32, 38, 52
Musée du Québec, No. 36
The National Gallery of Canada, Ottawa, Nos. 54, 59
Notman Photographic Archives, McCord Museum,
Montreal, No. i
Larry Ostrom, Art Gallery of Ontario, Nos. 56, 60, 61
Frances K. Smith, Kingston, Nos. 1, 4, 5, 10, 12
Gabor Szilasi, Montreal, Nos. 16, 22, 25, 27, 33, 34, 37,
39, 40, 41, 47, 48, 49, 50, 51, 55, 58
Roland Weber, Nos. 43A, B, C